CW01192787

The Transformation

Juliana Spahr

atelos
26

© 2007 by Juliana Spahr
ISBN 978-1-891190-26-1

First edition, fourth printing

The cover image is of the Leucaena leucocephala, also known as koa haole; photograph by G.D. Carr, from *Vascular Plant Family Access Page*, www.botany.hawaii.edu/faculty/mimos.htm. Used with permission.

ɫ Atelos
A Project of Hip's Road
Editors: Lyn Hejinian and Travis Ortiz
Design: Lyn Hejinian
Cover Design: Ree Katrak/Great Bay Graphics

Table of Contents

1, page 11

2, page 25

3, page 37

4, page 53

5, page 89

6, page 117

7, page 135

8, page 165

9, page 189

afterword, page 215

The Transformation

1

Flora and fauna grow next to and around each other without names. Humans add the annotation. They catalogue the flora and fauna, divide them up, chart their connections and variations, eventually name them, and as they do this they read into them their own stories. In 1569, a doctor who came from afar to the continent that has the Atlantic on one side and the Pacific on the other had what was called the maracujá vine and its elaborate flower pointed out by those who had been living for many generations on this continent. Forty years later a priest, also from afar, looked at the plant and saw within the flower the crucifixion, the five wounds of Christ, the crown of thorns, the cords that bound the body to the cross, the doubters, the goblet of the Last Supper, saw a story of Christ in a new world vine, and the vine got renamed the passiflora, the passionflower. The passiflora did not show up on the island in the middle of the Pacific, where this story—a story of a different them who also came from afar—takes place, until the late nineteenth century. But passiflora gets busy once it arrives. It grows towards the light and its leaves unfold like solar panels pointing towards the sun and then it begins to smother and break underlying vegetation with dense mats of stems and foliage. Those who lived on this island in the middle of the Pacific in the late nineteenth century did not see the story of Christ, or perhaps they did but it did not interest them. What was called the maracujá, the passiflora, the passionflower, they called the huehue haole. Huehue is the name of a climber native to the islands. Haole is the word that is used to describe some of them in this story, people who arrive from somewhere else. In the world of plants it is also used to describe a particularly noxious and invasive species.

This is a story of the passiflora and the tree canopy. This is a story of three who moved to an island in the middle of the Pacific together. This story begins when they all got on an airplane to fly to the island. In the plane, two sat in one row of two seats and one sat in a row ahead of the other two. The one who sat in a row ahead talked with another in the same row, someone whom they had just met, who had lived on an atoll for a number of years but now the atoll was gone because the ocean had risen above it. Together the three of them and the stranger who had lived on the atoll looked out the window of the plane and saw the island in the middle of the Pacific that would be their home. The island they saw was a mixture of green and of concrete and it was surrounded by water that was a deep blue. Out the window of the airplane, it looked like everything that they were told a tropical island might be. And when they got off the plane the air felt lush and was filled with the smells of plants and they felt their bodies embrace it.

They all carried their history with them on the airplane. Their history was like this . . . Two of them had been a couple for many years. This relationship was intense and variable and intellectually driven. One of them had met another. This relationship was intense and variable and passionate. Two of them had assumed that one of them would no longer be one of them. But it did not work out that way. No one broke up with anyone. Things just went on. And now one of them had taken a job on an island in the middle of the Pacific and the other two had to decide whether to move or not. They had met one afternoon in a bar and talked about the move. And there they decided to fix their relationship into a triangle. At the bar meeting it was awkward for them to talk. They felt uncomfortable and there was a lot of silence, but they decided anyway that they would all move to the island together. They liked each other and they admitted this. All of them learned from all of them. They all had their own interests and these interests intersected and overlapped with other interests and they all felt they could be shaped by each other into some new thing.

One of them would move from bed to bed; one would be always coupled; one would be single every other night. There was a pattern. And so each day they would have to think about which bed had been the bed for waking. Or which skin had been the most touched of the skins. What certain specific memory had been the most recent. What smell. What feeling. What satisfaction.

When they first landed they went from an airplane into a car and they went from a car into an empty apartment and then went from an empty apartment into a bar where they had beers in the afternoon. They were awkward because they got off the airplane on an island. They were awkward with their bodies in the five-hour time difference after a ten-hour flight. They were awkward because they had never lived together before.

Once they were on the island they had no words for themselves. They had only theories. And the words they thought they might use did not work. They did not know what to make of how it felt reassuring to watch on public television the female hedge sparrow vigorously shaking its tail feathers at two different male birds to indicate their desire to be inseminated by each of them in close succession or to watch a cable channel's documentary on a group who lived in the Amazon who married more than one person at a time, a group the documentary called the marrying tribe of the Amazon, or to watch the music channel's soap opera subplot of a girl and two guys who liked to have sex all together and who as a result agreed that the only ethical thing to do was to only have sex when all three were present, an agreement that was immediately broken by two of them when the third went off to study. The interest they felt in these images that came at them without their input made them feel stupid but they could find few models to turn to among those around them so they could not stop thinking about these models made for them by other people far away from them. Lack of understanding was all around. It defined them. They could not understand what the documentary called the marrying tribe. They did not even know the real name of the marrying tribe, the name that the members of the tribe had chosen to call themselves. The documentary used the term the marrying tribe.

In their apartment, they each had their own room. They lived their lives most fully in their own rooms. Most of their emotional life was experienced at their desks and they often interacted with each other from these desks through their computers. The desks that they had in each room were identical. They had made them together on the same day out of plywood. And the desk chairs were identical. They had gone together to the office warehouse store and they had bought three identical desk chairs with wheels and blue denim upholstery. They each had computers on their desks. Yet they kept their identical desk chairs at different heights. And they kept different sorts of things on their desks and their computers. One had papers and books strewn about in piles, abandoned birds nests, and several lamps. One had ashtrays and matches and voodoo dolls and candles. One had shells and weird materials found on the ground and math books.

As they worked at their desks, they wondered if they were a new pattern or a very old pattern that had fallen out of style and then been forgotten about. None of this thinking went much of anywhere. They wondered about this in the back of their brains, in the background of their daily thoughts. The front of their brains could not really see the pattern or make sense of it. They were aquarium fish who did not understand they were in a tank and there was nowhere to go. Among their desks, the day-to-day felt normal to them. They got up and made breakfast and then they went and did the things they did for work and then they would meet later in the day and eat dinner and then do the things that people did before they went to bed like read or watch something on television or just sit on the lanai talking. They thought of this as normal life. They just did it with the motion of moving between three instead of two.

Some of them were poets so they constantly rewrote metaphors to make them work for them. They did not want metaphors to matter but they had no other way of cloaking themselves in the normal. When talking to others, such as their parents, they kept resorting to metaphors of nature, as if that would make them natural. But the metaphors of nature always failed them. Everything happens somewhere in nature. For every polygamous hedge sparrow or fairy wren there were all those birds that mated for life. And the documentary on the life of birds cautioned that the extreme infidelity of hedge sparrows was not widespread among birds, should they identify too completely.

They avoided words to describe their relation because words felt wrong. And there were not any really. They heard rumors of there being words for their sort of relation in the language that was spoken on the island before the whaling ships arrived, but they could not speak this language. They asked a few people who spoke it about the words and these people did not know them. In their language all the words made them feel funny or dirty or untrue or part of a very traditional religion. Instead they just avoided words even as they often found it necessary to use metaphors. They tried to understand the balance of three-legged stools. The rules of triangles. The smoothness of three-point turns made by a new but practiced driver in a driver's education class. They tried to think of their desks and their lives as universals and particulars, as boundaries and ties, as locals and globals, as individualisms and collectivisms. They pictured the interconnected hubs of migration in the sea of islands. They had after all arrived by plane. And so they identified with planes. They did not like this part of themselves but it was a part of themselves anyway. And they took comfort in connections that also had individualism in them—the kolea's daytime claim to a certain plot of land and then the nighttime nesting in groups or the image they saw once on television of group skydiving, the sort where fifty or so people all dive at the same time and then try to join hands in a big radiating wheel while in free fall. The skydiving was hard to do, the group had to attempt many dives before they got it right. But once it was done, there was a center and then people radiating out; it was nonhierarchical in the vertical sense; everyone was on the same level; but some were closer to the center; everyone was touching, holding hands, and yet everyone had their own parachute.

As it is for all humans, many other humans interacted with them and they were grateful when their identical desks and chairs were seen as normal, as something that could be mentioned casually in conversation but did not need to be dwelled upon or would not make them confused or nervous. They were grateful even when a friend who lived on the continent gave them a copy of a film set amid the turbulence of World War I about a decades-long love triangle that both tests and strengthens the bond between the two men, even though two of them refused to watch it. They said it was because it had subtitles but the one of them who watched wished that they had not because it ends so badly. Another time they were grateful when a friend who had genealogical ties to the island from before the whaling ships arrived called late at night after drinking awa. The friend asked what it was like. The friend said they couldn't keep one relationship going. Even though they were not speaking well or lacked words they were grateful for the friend's late-at-night-after-drinking-awa call because they had a hard time telling others about who was what. There were awkward moments, moments that they did not yet really know how to deal with because they did not really know how to be confident in their relationship. There were those moments such as when one of them put down two names in the guest slot for the office holiday party and were told that only partners could come, not roommates. Or those moments where they had to reply, when someone invited them and their partner to dinner, that they had two partners. And although they frequently adopted a haughty tone and called themselves perverts when asked about their sexuality, they greatly feared appearing overly lecherous or perverse and as a result they abandoned all flirting and innuendo even though they had enjoyed flirting and innuendo a great deal when they were just one of a couple. And, they had to admit to themselves, they were not really perverts in the traditional sense. They were just an atypical relationship pattern in that there were three of them but very typical in that they more or less followed the codes of behavior and patterns of most married couples. They shared their money and they shared the chores and they ate breakfast and dinner together but not lunch and they went to the movies on weekend nights.

For a long time everything felt like airplanes to them. Like moving between. Like migration. Like motion. Not the way they imagined migration must feel to garden snakes or ants or slugs or plovers or monarchs or whales or any of the herds of walking animals that move with what they imagined was an inner smoothness, an instinct, a nameless desire that propelled them in a forward motion from one place to another. Instead they felt uprooted and tense around the shoulders and dry in the mouth and also full of tiredness and boredom. They felt like they were still breathing stale air and sitting in awkward seats. They felt like sudden drops in altitude and turbulence might happen at any moment but that if they just held on and relaxed it would most likely be okay.

In this place, on the island in the middle of the Pacific, there were other new patterns of relating. They felt stroked by the weather that was unusually pleasant. But they felt lost otherwise. This was not necessarily because of the new patterns of their relationship but more because of the new patterns that the history of the island left on their relationships with others. This is mainly the story of how the history of the island changed them, the story of the huehue haole and the tree canopy. It cannot help but also be a story about how they were shaped by perhaps being and perhaps not being perverts, but still it is more a story about three of them who moved to an island that was not theirs. While this could be a little-grass-shack story with a 'ukelele and a palm tree, they were lovers of desks and they were trying to be like the finches who grew new and different beaks in reaction to the wide variety of microclimates on the island, yet they still tried to keep their love of connection in the front of their minds. So this is a story of three who moved to an island in the middle of the Pacific and how it changed them. And a story of how they became aware they were a they in the cruel inquisitive sense, in the sense of not being a part of us or we, in the sense of accusation, whether they wanted to be they or not. It is a story about realizing that they cannot shrug off this they and so a story of trying to think with it. A story of how much this realization of being a they changed them and a story of embracing this change. It is also a story of debt. A story of how the island made them recognize themselves as they and then how this recognition caused them to write with endless qualifiers and doubts and an attendant absurdity and how they enjoyed this recognition and its absurdity because it felt like so much more information. They thought of themselves as taking on this they, as if they had decided to join those who buy and then wear proudly a t-shirt with a word such as cunt or queer or the name of a certain place of birth that is often said in insult printed across the front of it in larger letters. And so perhaps it is a story of coming to an identity, coming to realize that they not only had a gender that was decided for them without their consent and by historical events that they had not even been alive to witness, but they also had a race and a sexuality that was decided for them without their consent and by historical events that they had not even been alive to witness and they just had to deal with this. So it is also a story of finding an ease in discomfort. And a catalogue of discomfort. And as it is a story of what they talked about when they sat together on the lanai late at night talking, it is also a story about living with theys. A story of how they felt at these moments on the lanai as if they were coral and they could spawn by talking, by talking into the night. A story of how they felt as if they were milkweed. As if there was an impingement, an attachment that grew out of them that scattered bits of them outwards into the wind and then there they were fluttering, moving, and scattering. As if they not only sent seeds out into the wind but they also had pistil heads, shrouded by fused anthers, which served as landing platforms for pollinators who would come over to suck nectar from their filament hoods. As if they were the milkweed and also as if they were the butterfly that might arrive and move about, let their leg slip into a groove between the anthers of the milkweed where a saddlebag-like packet of pollen might be waiting. Then when they, the butterfly they, visited the next flower, the saddlebag would be deposited into a receptive stigmatic slit on the side of the pistil head and the pollen they carried would burst out of their bags. A story of how they were they as if they were a root and they could each cut from the root a sucker and then pull this sucker from the ground and transplant it in a dark soil so that a new shoot would grow. A story of how they were a spawning mullet-they, traveling through tidal zones searching for food, who guzzles up a seed-they which lodges in the mullet-they's stomach. And then a story of how they were a sooty storm petrel-they who eats the mullet-they and thus the seed-they and then passes the seed-they as excreta into a muddy bank-they in another part of the ocean-they. So they were, they are, defined by the just accusations of others and intimate with one another inside this accusation.

2

The minute they got off the plane, they realized that the beauty of the island was its own radiant thing full of boths and that they had to begin with these boths. It was an island of both great environmental beauty and of great environmental destruction. And these boths fed each other in a complicated feedback loop. Because the island was so beautiful, so full of lush canyon valleys, of broad and green mountain slopes, of low-lying and marshy planes, of sandy and sparsely vegetated shores, of sharp and dark lava areas, it was so troubled, so invaded, so at risk. It had one of the highest rates of species extinction. And it had both calming and powerful winds. It had both dramatic hills and lush valleys. It had both clear, warm ocean waters that lapped modestly at the shore and clear, warm ocean waters that came roaring in with crisp and spectacular waves. When they looked around most of what they saw among the many things growing, flying, and crawling had been brought onto the island after the whaling ships arrived. It told a story of beauty and a story of mismanagement. It told a story of invasion and of acceptance as if it could tell both of these stories using the same vocabulary.

The longer they lived on the island, the more they learned. Not only about themselves but also about the island. On the island in the Pacific their eyes zoomed in a lot. They arrived in a plane and the plane swooped down and their mind swooped down with the plane and then they got out and they looked at the world with the vision of swooping down, with the vision of detail. They looked at the plants of the island with great interest and fell into the parts of them. They fell into the roots and the leaves and the stems. They fell into the blade and the petiole. They fell into the buds, the nodes, and the leaf scars. They fell into pinnate, palmate, parallel, or dichotomous. They fell into deep green and velvety, into rich panoply, into undulating tapestry and valley breeze, into odors of extreme delicacy and pervasiveness.

They rarely widened their perspective or used their peripheral vision. They went for days without noticing the horizon. Everything was all detail and specificity. Everything was local. They learned that the place to which they had moved was one island among one hundred and thirty-two in the earth's longest island chain. They learned that the ocean that surrounded the island where they lived spans over one third of the earth's surface and contains twenty-five thousand islands. They learned that there might be as many as one thousand two hundred languages in the ocean and that one large especially rocky island in the ocean had close to eight hundred alone. Often they heard it said that this was a problem or a limitation that the people who lived on the islands must overcome. The societies on these islands are too segregated they heard some say; they mimic the geography; they can never get along these people; and thus they cannot govern themselves, others need to do it; or thus their literatures are of limited scope and applicability; because there is an excess of specificity, there is an excess of dependency and a lack of development or maybe even a lack of radicalness. But whenever they heard this they thought also of how this expanse of salt water was not necessarily a separation but could also be a connective fluid. They thought of travel, trade, and migration. They thought of canoes and of jets. They also thought of the land snails that might have arrived to the island by a prehistoric chain of steppingstone islands. And they thought of the honeycreepers—the 'i'iwi and the 'apapane and the 'ākohekohe—who lived on the island before humans arrived yet no one knew how they got there because the birds were incapable of flying between islands. They thought of the koa with its wide, expansive canopy and how the koa's nearest relative was over five thousand miles away. They thought of how hurricane winds carry spores, seeds, and insects. And they thought of the migratory paths of the ruddy turnstone, the wandering tattlers, the sanderling, the pintail duck, and the shoveler duck. They did not think up these things on their own. They thought of them because they learned them from others. A novelist from another small island in this ocean, for instance, pointed out at a conference the difference between seeing what surrounded them as islands in a far sea, tiny dots of land separated by wide expanses of ocean, or as a sea of islands, which implied a more holistic perspective in which the ocean and islands are joined.

Because the air and the things in the air and the land and the things upon the land were so wonderful, so thick with detail, so solid with color their small brains were unable to understand it as at risk of going away. Or what it meant that so many spectacular parts of it had already been lost. This was because it was so much more wonderful in terms of nature than other places they had lived. They were limited by their ability to envision it because the land in the places where they had grown up had always been defined by the development and industry that was creating the hole in the ozone, the disappearing atolls, and all the plastics that were collecting in the ten million square miles of still water that was surrounded by the north Pacific subtropical gyre. The beauty of the island was so intense and so variable that it entered into their brain as a drug and they were high on it and only able to see it as intense and wonderful. The intense and the wonderful was so big that it took up all the space at the front of their brain and as a result they had trouble seeing it as at risk and colonized.

But the real story the back of their brains kept reminding them was the story of the huehue haole and the tree canopy. They were newcomers to the island but they were at the same time part of a long history of arrival to the island. The island was contested land. There were those who had arrived a long time before the whaling ships arrived and they set up a complicated and nuanced culture. Then the whaling ships arrived and a history of overthrow and occupation by those who, like them, arrived from the continent began. Those who, like them, had arrived from the continent had arrived many years ago and set up their own form of government, an inefficient and unfair one, and had outlawed certain forms of dance and also the language that was spoken on the island before the whaling ships had arrived. This history was a history that had happened over and over in many different places. It was not specific to the island in the middle of the Pacific. But on the island in the middle of the Pacific, despite how this specific history had happened many years ago, it was still a fresh history that was remembered by everyone on the islands.

They were a part of this history of occupation because of where they were born and it remained with them and was inescapable in most daily interactions. Even though they had for years seen themselves as distinct from the government that currently occupied the continent and the islands, here on the island in the middle of the Pacific they had no ability to pretend that they were occupied. Instead they were seen as occupiers. It was with them in line at the grocery store and while waiting for the light to change at the intersection. It was with them when they walked down the streets and when they met people in a bar. All around them were reminders of what they were and of their impact. They lived among plants that grew into each other in various and unique ways. There was not only the huehue haole that smothered shrubs, small trees, and the ground layer. But there was the scrubby koa haole that formed dense thickets and excluded all other plants. And the kamani haole and the wiliwili haole and the laua'e haole. Most of the birds they saw around them came from other places and took over. The myna was introduced in 1865 to control army worms. The sparrow was introduced in 1871. The Japanese white eye was introduced in 1929. The red-billed leiothrix probably escaped from a cage in 1911. As the birds changed, the plants changed with them from native to largely alien because the birds carried seeds in their feathers and in their waste. There was an indigenous bird, the kōlea, that summered on the continent and wintered on the island. It was often called the haole bird because it came to the island, got fat, and then returned to the continent.

This history, this history of occupation, swooped down and then took away what they thought they were and replaced it with a weak complicity that they did not like about themselves but had to accept even as they tried to speak out against it in their tiny ineffectual voices, tried to say that they too felt occupied. When they first arrived, that the place was colonized unnerved them.

At first they thought they never wanted to live in a place that was colonized. Then they began to realize that it was hard to find a place that had not been colonized by someone at some time. They had after all been born on a colonized continent. So then they decided that they did not want to live in a place that was recently colonized. Or a place that identified as colonized. But after they lived in this colonized place for a while, they became obsessed with other colonized places. They became colonialism groupies. They read colonial and postcolonial novels avidly. They searched out films from other colonized places, mailing away for them from distribution centers on the continent. They listened to dancehall and reggae music. They looked at clogging in a new light. They read history, sociology, botany, literary criticism. As long as it was about how one people dominated another people, it felt relevant to their lives. Books that they had been made to read in graduate school and had found irrelevant to their thinking about avant-garde poetry suddenly felt crucial. A friend would talk about their mother's schizophrenia and refer to the work of an intellectual who came from a colonized place and wrote movingly about this and it would feel real and make sense in a way that it would not have five years earlier. They began to think they might now understand a friend they had hung out with when they had lived for a year on another island in the Pacific, an island that had also been repeatedly colonized and now was divided in two. This friend had stickers that said one nation on their moped and their notebook and their cellphone but was always saying that they hated the other part of the island because it had no discos. At the end of one of the films that they got from the distribution center on the continent, a character made a speech about nationalism and tradition being respectful of women. When they heard this speech they felt a small thrill that nationalism could be progressive even though they knew the history of nationalisms to be a complicated one and did not understand the politics of this other nation and felt nervous about relating too strongly to nationalisms from places they knew little about. This same thrill took the form of goosebumps at local protests when one part of the crowd began chanting i ku mau mau and another part answered i ku wa. And certain songs and chants on the radio would also give them chills, especially ones of regaining the land. This chill came over them even though these nationalisms and their films and songs were not for them as those to whom they had genealogical ties had only taken land, not had land taken from them. This chill they thought was probably about the sudden possibility of escape from large systemic limitations. They too were trying to escape from large systems, from limitations on relation, which is probably why these songs and chants on the radio about regaining the land that had no direct relation to their lives felt so thrilling. They were guilty they realized of misunderstanding the songs and chants if songs and chants meant to indict them and those like them, those from afar, induced nothing more than goose bumps. But the goose bumps were involuntary. Although they did not know it at the time, this issue of how art and music and literature took root in their body and induced certain involuntary reactions, how art and music and literature might cause tiny muscles at the base of each hair to contract and thus pull the hair erect, would come to dominate their concerns for years to come. And while they had never indulged in the misunderstanding that art and music and literature could be independent of politics, the goosebumps were a reminder that they had a lot to learn about how art and music and writing not only raised the hair on their arms but also altered their consciousness.

They talked about these things and they talked about other things that filled them with the patheticness of their inaction amongst themselves at the breakfast table in the morning or on the lanai at night. They talked about how it was announced on the television news that one of the poles of the earth that had been frozen for many years was now a giant melting puddle. They talked about how the ocean was huge and it was filled with ʻoʻopu and ʻalaʻihi and ʻūʻū and limu and plastic. It was so huge and so all around them that it was scary to think about. And then even scarier to think some more about it rising. They talked some about the pool of melting but cool water on the pole. And then some more of the atoll that was no longer an atoll. They talked about the islands that were disappearing under water. They talked about the documentary they had seen about an atoll in the southern part of the Pacific that had been the home of about a thousand people for many years. The atoll had a special source of clear, crisp water on it and this water had allowed these thousand people to live on it. This water had soothed many parched tongues and had cooled the forehead of many who were feverish and cleaned many bodies of sweat and dirt. It had cultivated many crops. But now the atoll was under water, under saltwater. The documentary showed the legs of someone who had been born on the atoll when it was above water as they walked slowly across the atoll and the four feet of water that covered it. This water that covered the atoll was clear and warm and the stunning blue color that water takes on close to the equator. Small, colorful fish swam by their legs. They talked about how it was both beautiful and horrible. They wondered together if there could be a word for this fearful symmetry in any language. A word for this emotion that combined intense, awful loss with a recognition of continuing and endless beauty despite, perhaps even caused by, the loss. It was an emotion they had felt a lot as a child when they would drive by the chemical factories south of where they lived in the middle of the continent. They were so mesmerized by the million different lights and the billowing smokestacks that they would beg their parents to wake them up before they drove by if they happened to fall asleep. This recognition of human-induced horrible beauty caused talk also about what it meant to be part of the place that uses the most energy. The place most responsible for the growth in the ozone hole that was growing over islands that were far away from this place. The place that had recently withdrawn from an international accord that had proposed limiting the emissions that caused the ozone hole and had absurdly blamed developing nations for the hole. The place that was bombing other places right now so as to be able to continue playing a leading role in the melting of ice caps. And the place also responsible for the bombing of various nearby islands in this island chain. They talked about citizenship in an occupied land. Then this led to talk about the extinction of species, which had a special relevance as more species were dying on the island they had moved to than anywhere else. And they talked also about how it was predicted that 25 percent of the earth's species were likely to vanish by 2050. And they talked of how smog was causing sunlight to diminish on the planet from 10 to 37 percent depending on whether one lived in a more remote area or in a more urban area. And they talked of the rise of the H5N1 flu. And they talked some more of the ten-million-square-mile mass of plastic waste in the north Pacific subtropical gyre.

3

The politics of the island were more complicated than the boths of the beauty of the island. The politics were not really built around boths but instead around the one or the other. The politics were something else altogether. They were a part of the island that bit into them and those around them with bladelike, piercing mouthparts that stabbed through the skin and then injected a saliva that teemed with digestive enzymes, viruses, and anticoagulants. This bite often left behind an annoying itch, a reminder that things were not both the one and the other, could not be both the one and the other because both made no sense because there could not be both colonialism and sovereignty. The uncomfortable itch did not last long, but the bite left in their bloodstream a troubling, a questioning, some new sort of information, some prickly new cells that attached themselves to their blood cells and reshaped them, something that their immune system had to deal with that it hadn't dealt with before. This thing that entered into their bloodstream changed them. It was not that these prickly new cells made them sick. Instead it was as if they were in the world of science fiction and the cells were a new mutant spawn that changed them into another sort of being as they entered into a symbiotic relationship with them. It was as if there were a pre-infection state where they thought of themselves as progressive, as part of the solution, and a postinfection state where they saw themselves as part of the problem. As if they became infected with something that quietly added genetic material to all parts of their body as it slowly mutated all of their cells into some other shape. These prickly new cells would show up in any blood test from now on and they would pass them on to those they had intimate contact with and after years they and those around them would be different people as a result.

As the months went by, they found themselves thinking with this new information in their bloodstream about how to negotiate things, about analogy, about the word we, about how to be in a place where they could not escape from being representative of the government that currently occupied the continent and the islands no matter how much they hated this government and felt that it did the things that it did without their consent or approval. We was undeniably a contested word for them. They often felt too large in it, too large because there were three of them instead of two. But too large in other ways also. One of them had moved to the island in the middle of the Pacific to work at the university. At the orientation to their job at the university they were in a room full of people from afar of many different races and nationalities and all of them were told at this meeting that they had three options, they could be a haole, a stupid haole, or a stupid fucking haole. This was the first of many moments where it was pointed out to them that they were not from the island in the middle of the Pacific and that they were there on the island only because of a history of imperialism and colonialism that favored them.

The university cast a large shadow of the one or the other over all that happened there. Shortly after they arrived one of them went to a rally at the university that was protesting the latest round of budget cuts. On the island in the middle of the Pacific, the budget-cut protest, like most budget-cut protests, turned quickly from a budget-cut protest to a protest about other things. The protest became about the hiring practices of the university, which hired almost exclusively people from various continents and very few people from any islands, not only few from the one on which the university was located but also few from any of the other islands in the Pacific. At the protest, a student leader who had genealogical ties to the island from before the whaling ships arrived gave a speech that began with the budget cuts but then concluded with an offer to buy any haole professor who wanted one a one-way ticket off the island. When they heard this speech at first they cringed. They cringed not because they were angry. It was instead a cringe of recognition. A cringe that the university did not hire fairly and that they themselves had gotten their job because of the unfair hiring practices of the university. They cringed because they agreed and because they agreed they longed to go up to the student leader after the talk and ask for their ticket back to someplace. But then they wondered to what place? What would be the proper destination for the ticket? Did they belong on the continent, where they had been born? But they were in some sense as new to the continent as they were to the island in the middle of the Pacific. They and their parents had been born on the continent, but none of their parents' parents had been born there and the continent too had a history of arrival by people from afar who came and acted as if the place was theirs.

This was just one reminder among many. There were all sorts of pressures around writing and the island. And the pressure came from all over. When they had first decided to move to the island, a friend who lived on the continent had said to them that they hoped that they were not going to turn into this other person, a person who like them had come to the island from afar and now carried the prickly new cells in their body and as a result of the cells now were infected with a commitment to write about and publish the work of writers of the island.

But that sort of snide pressure not to write about the island was nothing next to what was said at times by those who had genealogical ties to the island from before the whaling ships arrived. Once they went to a reading at the university by a poet with genealogical ties to the island from before the whaling ships arrived. The poet sang songs and played guitar and read poems that compared those from afar to greedy white pigs. In the middle of the reading the poet announced that they hated haoles, although they clarified, not as much as their brother, who really hated haoles and would not even talk to them. The poet admitted that they hated the university also. But, the poet added, the university was the only place that ever invited them to read and when they read at the university, mainly haoles showed up to listen, so there they were once again, the poet said with some resignation, reading to haoles. Then they next read a poem that was about an acquired immune deficiency syndrome and in place of the words acquired immune deficiency syndrome they used the word haole. They did this, they explained, because it was haoles who brought the acquired immune deficiency syndrome to the island in the middle of the Pacific.

At other moments they would find themselves in their office listening to a friend who was a student, a friend also like them from afar but from a small island nation in the Pacific with a long history of occupation by other nations, talk about how they would never fuck a haole. Haole pussy, they would declaim, was snapping-turtle pussy, or they would talk about how haoles looked sickly with their unattractive white skin.

At other times, they would go to meetings held at the university to discuss how to end the colonization of the island and at these meetings someone often got up and said that haoles should not drive this anticolonial bus; haoles should sit at the back of the bus.

Basically, their overall response to all of this the one or the other was ineffectual and often naïve. They negotiated through all this by flailing about and contradicting themselves. Perhaps the poet, they would first think, might want to think more about the question of how their poetry shaped their audience. Then the next moment they would note how the poet who hated haoles was unusually gentle with children, even haole children, and so they would say oh they are just crazy and they say crazy things so as to not take the poet's perhaps legitimate hatred of haoles seriously. Then they would admit that the poet was probably partially right, that haoles probably did bring the acquired immune deficiency syndrome to the island because most of the people who came to the island from afar were haoles. And they would next claim to be intellectually interested in how the poem reversed the accusation that was often made by those on the whaling ships that the people, especially the women who were on the island when the whaling ships arrived, were sexually promiscuous. Then they would notice the poem's myopia, the absence in the poem of a larger history of the syndrome, how it infected so many people of so many different races from so many different places, and the absence of the political movements that had insisted on a nuanced and complicated awareness of the acquired immune deficiency syndrome. Then they would think about what it felt to be associated with a disease that was often transmitted through intimate contact and what it felt to be of an identity category that was called sexually predatory and diseased, something that they felt sensitive about already as they perhaps were and yet perhaps were not perverts. And then they would notice how their mind raced to avoid this association and began to make elaborate complaints about how the poem was medically inaccurate and then how their mind moved from medically inaccurate to medically dangerous because it might suggest that as long as they did not indulge in snapping-turtle pussy that they could not get the acquired immune deficiency syndrome.

Similarly with their friend who talked endlessly about snapping-turtle pussy. Their first reaction was to just flail about, to internalize the comment and then to defend themselves, to say to themselves that they did not have snapping-turtle pussy, their pussy did not bite, and then to call the friend sexist. And then they would back up and marvel that their friend, who never got any pussy and yet wanted some a great deal perhaps more than they wanted most other things in life, was so confident that their complaint was not with haole culture or haole politics but was with haole pussy. Or they would say to themselves that their friend who claimed to hate haole pussy was less a scary misogynist and more just yet another person made crazy by the difficulties of childhood immigration to the island in the middle of the Pacific, so crushed by these difficulties that they confused haole government with haole pussy.

While the back-of-the-bus metaphor often shocked them as it kept coming up again and again, it shocked them a little less each time. But still they felt troubled with how the metaphor confused slavery's history with haole privilege or how it made somewhat false comparisons between colonization and slavery and yet the comparisons, they next thought, were also somewhat true because colonization and slavery were both systems where one group of people took over another group of people and denied their status as fully human in the name of things like economic gain.

What they realized about themselves was that most often they dismissed the thinking. They dismissed it in as many different ways as they could. They dismissed it by not taking it seriously and saying it was a performance and by taking it seriously and saying it was insane. They moved between these positions and occasionally threw in other positions such as the position of taking it all seriously and leaving. Every time this idea popped up then they thought to themselves that they did not know where to go. And so then they would hammer this idea down and back up would pop the performance explanation. They would hammer that down and the crazy explanation would pop back up. It was an elaborate game of anxiety-ridden whack-a-mole.

At other moments, their dismissal took the form of a performance for them. They performed their coolness, they performed how they could take it whenever they heard haole go home called out at a protest. They could take it and they did not get angry and did not complain about being oppressed. They could stand behind the words haole go home and nod their head and say yes, they should go home. And they could be friends with they who said I hate haoles or haole go home or haole pussy is snapping-turtle pussy. And these friendships made them feel superior to those who could not take it and who developed a sort of reductive anger and constant frown and rigidity to their body as a result. They felt superior. They felt less haole if they could stand up and take them saying I hate haoles and nod their heads and say yes. And they often joined up with other haoles who felt that they too could take it to form a coalition of haoles who could take it, haoles who were friends with those who said I hate haoles. And there was a smug self-satisfaction in their ability to nod their heads when they said I hate haoles that let them look down on those with the reductive anger and constant frown.

And at other moments they did not dismiss. Instead they decided to learn from these moments, learn what it meant to be they in the accusative. In their own house each of them were changed in different ways as the prickly new accusative they took over more and more of their bodies. One of them stopped writing because writing got too fraught with cultural politics and instead they bought postcards of men and women posing seductively in bikini bathing suits on various beaches of the island and small stickers of fish and teddy bears and flowers and other such things and suggestively applied them to the images of men and women on the postcards. Another of them just got lost in the tourism industry. They made jokes about how the only place they felt at home was among the concrete skyscrapers and they went to work making mai tais in a pool bar. The pool bar was filled with people from afar who had saved their money and flown many miles to experience a tropical vacation filled with pristine beaches and gentle waves and cool breezes. The waves were gentle and the breezes were cool but the beaches were filled with imported sand and twenty-story hotels and it was hard for those who came from afar even to find a space on the imported sand to spread their towel. The pool bar was thus a place where those from afar went to drink with crushed expectations and they served them mai tais with a sense of responsibility and listened to the stories of despair that were induced by the crushed expectations caused by the beaches of imported sand and twenty-story hotels. And the other of them turned to writing nature poems about the place where they wrote poems about the beauty of the island and listed all the names of the plants and animals in poems in the language that was on the island before the whaling ships arrived and then they took these nature poems and translated the parts of them that were in the language that arrived on the island with the whaling ships back and forth between various other languages that arrived in various parts of the Pacific with the whaling ships using a computer program they found on the internet so that the poems no longer resembled nature poems and the beauty of the plants and animals was lost in the fragmented mistranslations.

And while they did these things, this question of what it meant to be the accusative they still defined many parts of their day for them and they still felt as if they were caught in their flailing and contradicting. So they often looked at what those who came from afar did, those who were willing to take the accusative they into their bodies and let it change them. They noticed that some of them devoted themselves to learning the language that had existed on the island before the whaling ships arrived so as to better understand the island. Some of them invited writers from the island into the university to speak. Some of them changed their research focus after they arrived on the island and they wrote books that they could not have written without learning from the island. Some of them edited collections where issues that defined the island were debated. Some of them embraced grassroots organizing and they handed out flyers and curated speaker series. Some of them formed a reading group to educate themselves about the island. And some of them marched in protests and gave talks at the protests about why haoles should be supportive of sovereignty for the island.

Negotiating this accusative they not only changed them and their bodies, but it also changed their thought patterns. They liked this change and once they realized this, they cultivated and provoked this change in various ways. For instance, several of them had formed a reading group to further provoke this change in their thought patterns and they eagerly joined it. At the reading group, they read articles that stimulated debates about what they should do with their bodies on the island in a musty, windowless room. The debate that they indulged in was a very old debate but they acted as if no one had ever had this debate before and in the musty windowless room at the university they rarely made references to anything outside of the island. It was as if the ocean that surrounded the island sequestered their thinking and any attempt that they made to float away on a raft of photocopied articles was foiled by the high surf that surrounded the island, which would toss them and their raft of photocopied articles back onto the rocks that surrounded the shore. It was not that they lacked topics for debate in the musty, windowless room. It was the opposite. The island had so many issues for them to debate that they were constantly overwhelmed by their insufficient knowledge of the island and its rich culture and history before the whaling ships arrived and its rich history and culture after the whaling ships arrived. They were never under the delusion that they could acquire mastery of the subject. Still they debated among themselves the obligation of writing and art to the island in the middle of the Pacific, the differences between nationalism and ethnic nationalism and which defined what sorts of writing and art, the boundaries of the unreliable narrator and if this narrator turns its reader to enlightenment or if it just ends up perpetuating the very thing it meant to oppose, whether they had the right to impose rules or limits on writing and art, whether multivalence and complication made writing and art a stronger ally to a cause or a weaker one, whether an avant-garde practice that used fragmentation, quotation, disruption, disjunction, agrammatical syntax, and so on opened the mind or just befuddled it, whether the awakening that they felt from an avant-garde that used fragmentation, quotation, disruption, disjunction, agrammatical syntax, and so on was so resonant to them because they were from afar or if this resonance was also one that those who were born on the island in the middle of the Pacific also felt. It was by debating their conflicts on these issues and by consistently changing their minds and adapting their positions to the new information that they learned from the debates and from the photocopied articles that they came to a sort of friendship with each other in the reading group that was defined by controversy and not by agreement. And they began to see the fights about writing and art with friends as one crucial arena that might contain insight on this issue of what to do with their bodies on the island in the middle of the Pacific. They were all guilty of taking writing and art seriously and of taking it seriously even while they all knew that they had huge blind spots about the history of the island in the middle of the Pacific that no amount of reading photocopied articles and discussing them in a musty, windowless room at the university could fix.

If their dealings with the university were defined by the one or the other, once they walked off the campus life resonated with various shades and colors and the risk was not that they had to choose between the one or the other but that all the colors would merge into something indistinct and muddy. They talked about race all day long still off the campus of the university but with a lightness and an ease. In yoga class their teacher who was from afar, from a small island nation in the Pacific with a long history of occupation by other nations, would mock the other students when they did a pose well, asking the other students if they were willing to let a haole do the pose better than them. Or a friend who had genealogical ties to the island from before the whaling ships arrived would tease them about the genetic mutation that made them easily get sunburned. They in turn mocked their friend about always being late, about setting their clock so that it ran on those who had genealogical-ties-to-the-island-from-before-the-whaling-ships-arrived time. Or this friend would call them potato head and ask if they got potatoes with their plate lunch today and then when they said they got rice and they would then ask them if they had mixed in any mayonnaise with it. When they went out to eat, another friend, one born on the island but whose parents came from afar, told the joke that they can always tell the haoles at the Chinese restaurant because they are the ones not sharing their food. And then they would in turn poke at their friend saying that their idea of a funny joke had a Portuguese in it or their idea of fancy meal was spam. And then their friend would ask them if they heard that joke on Hawaii Five-0 and in response tell the one about how haoles think that having an open mind means dating a Canadian.

The joking about race was an accepted part of daily life, a way many different people dealt with being a they. And one of the stories that the island told about itself was that it was a place where they maintained their culture and everyone made fun of everyone else's equally. The story suggested a peculiar model of harmony, one in which a number of people attempt to expel the tensions around the categories of race and culture, tensions and categories that are imposed on them by imperialism, by mocking them. And while they appreciated this resistance strategy, appreciated the chance to joke about race, they also worried that it was easy to look at all the joking and miss the lingering effects of the imperial imposition. It was easy to celebrate all that was unique about the island in the middle of the Pacific, all that only happened there, the particular creole that those who were born on the island spoke or the special way of tuning a guitar so that it was turned to notes lower than was usual, and overlook the imposition's patterns of unequal exchanges, the way that imperial culture forced itself on the culture that was on the island before the whaling ships arrived and in response the culture that was on the island before the whaling ships arrived adapted and negotiated and mixed and reconfigured but the imperial culture did not let the culture that was on the island before the whaling ships arrived shape it all that much. So they felt that the one or the other that all those debates in the musty, windowless room at the university pointed out to them was something that mattered and that no amount of jokes could cover over how it mattered.

As a result, they were constantly unsure if it was more ethical to just make their self smaller and quieter or whether they should speak out loudly about how wrong the history of the place was and risk getting told to sit down and shut up because their place of birth made them part of the problem no matter what, even if they sat at the back of the bus.

4

Basically, this question of what they were complicit with, a question that arose so clearly with the student's offer to buy any haole professor a one-way ticket off the island, took over so much of their brain not only because it mattered, because it told them something about the place in which they lived, but also because they worked for the university, and although they worked for a local university, a university that was mainly for people who lived on the island in the middle of the Pacific and was funded by their taxes, it was a part of a large university complex and so was also funded by the government from afar that currently occupied the island and because they worked for this national educational complex they constantly felt caught.

Before they arrived on the island in the middle of the Pacific, they had worked hard to get a job in this complex somewhere, anywhere. In order to become qualified for this job they had studied for many years and then had spent many more years of writing and revising and publishing articles and books that had no audience, books that were written in such an obscure manner about such minutia that they could only be of interest to a few fellow humans who also worked in the complex. And then it had taken them many years of job applications and interviews to get a job. They had applied for so many jobs, written so many letters, talked to so many different people about their teaching and their scholarship and their writing, that they could no longer really count the numbers. They guessed that they had applied for at least five hundred jobs and then had gone to at least forty hour-long interviews and then after that they had gone to at least twenty one- or two-day-long interviews with talks and meetings and lunches and dinners at various parts of the complex across the continent before they got this one job offer on the island in the middle of the Pacific. They had worked on this getting a job in the complex day in and day out for so long because at the time they had felt that working for the complex was somehow less coercive than most jobs because it didn't really involve selling things or making things for people to buy but also because they had at the time believed that education was transformation, believed that reading was a good thing, believed in literature's power to comfort, to reform, to stir the emotions, to offer guidance. They thought they were doing good by working in the complex. That they could be a little less guilty, maybe even a little more innocent, than if they worked in advertising or in the military-industrial complex.

They were the sort of person who worked hard at things; thus the relentless applications. But the endless applying for jobs was somewhat disorientating. They were not convinced that they deserved a job; but neither were they convinced that they did not deserve a job. That was how they thought of jobs in the complex, that they were something that had to be deserved. And they moved back and forth constantly between insecurity and hubris as they thought about whether they deserved a job or not. They applied for jobs in the complex with a vacant look on their face, a dissociated look, and they used any reasoning they could to just keep going forward and when they tripped over this issue of deserving they just got up and continued stumbling forward. One minute they would keep going forward by thinking of the generally kind people in the complex as idiots and they would say to themselves that there are so many idiots in this complex that they might as well be one of them. And the next minute they would think that their work was good, or maybe not good but at least was decent enough, that they did deserve, that they were as good as the idiots. But then the next minute they would trip and look at their work with the clear eyes of disrespect and they would notice the smallness of their ideas, too small even for a complex that valued small ideas and bitter arguments about minutia. And then the next minute they would be overwhelmed with respect for their colleagues and their devotion to the smallness of ideas and the slow-moving nature of their thought in a time that valued bold sketches and quick-moving ideas; they, their colleagues, were true rebels, they would think, as they devoted their lives to the life of the mind when the rest of the world valued superficial sparkles that numbed the mind.

When they had been in graduate school, they had tried to understand the complex by compulsively collecting rules about what to write about and what not to write about, about how faculty members must be of a certain rank to be on dissertation committees, about where to publish and where not to publish. They slowly realized it was better to go to a school funded by private individuals rather than state governments, and it was especially good to go to one of the schools that were among the first established on the continent. It was better to have advisors who were themselves players in the complex than to have advisors who were serious scholars but who did not know many people in the complex. It was better not to publish than to publish in journals the complex did not approve of. Those who were successful in the complex more often than not had family members in the complex. Dissertations should not be about a single author, and yet they should not stray too far from a single nation or historical period, and should not mix literatures from too many different languages, and should have a thirty-page theoretical introduction that laid out certain problems or questions and this section could, perhaps even should, use theoretical writing written in the late seventies as long as the theorists were from the continent across the Atlantic, and it could, perhaps should, use highly elliptical and awkward language as long as this was done in the name of theory from the continent across the Atlantic, but it should not do this in the name of art. The list of rules went on and on. There were rules about identities and genders and rules about sentence structures and tense and voice and emotion. Rules about what they could and could not be, rules about choosing between being a poet or a critic. They added to these rules and revised them as times and fashions changed and while they were in graduate school they discussed them with their peers endlessly over and over late into the night at parties that were held in rundown apartments filled with furniture found on the street. They even had meetings with advisors who would give them their own versions of the rules and they would write these rules down in their notebook and then quote them back at one of the endless parties they went to as a graduate student where they would digest them with others, adding some of them to their own list of rules and rejecting others by complaining bitterly and unfairly about how their advisor wanted to oppress them with an outdated and conservative notion of the profession.

But despite their collecting and cataloguing of rules, they were for some reason unable to follow them. This probably had something to do with the peculiar form of disassociation they cultivated. After some time, they began to think of themselves as zombies in the complex. They mimicked the humans in the complex. They walked straight ahead, going forward. Sometimes they tripped and when they tripped, they just got up and continued stumbling forward. While they often fooled those not in the complex into thinking they belonged to the complex, they knew it was completely obvious to those in the complex that they did not belong. Those in the complex noticed the dumbstruck zombie expression on their face, the way they kept their head rigid and looked straight ahead as they kept walking forward until they ran into something and then stuck there, kept moving their legs as if walking although they were no longer moving forward. Or perhaps they noticed the rotten flesh on the front of their shirt that they, the zombie they, had not noticed because as a zombie they were not repulsed by the rotten flesh and in fact sort of liked having it around them on the front of their shirt.

They were not rebels. They did not rebel against the complex in a way that might matter, a way that might make them a romantic figure. They were not the well-dressed, aristocratic, intellectual vampire. Nor were they the freethinking, transformative, and slightly sexy werewolf. They were the zombie, straight ahead and dumb and a little gross; they were unable to follow the rules despite their hours inventorying them.

As they kept walking straight ahead with this vacant look on their face, they wrote seminar papers on writing that used fragmentation, quotation, disruption, disjunction, agrammatical syntax, and so on and they also published many poems and essays in various small journals with minute readerships and insisted on this writing as part of their work, as they phrased it in job interviews, adding a special vocal emphasis on the word work so as to indicate possible quotation marks around it, part of their cultural work. And even though the complex had, like all complexes, fairly rigorously defined but rarely directly spoken rules about dress that were perfectly obvious to them and which they could list if anyone had asked them to articulate them at one of those late-into-the-night graduate student parties held each weekend in rundown apartments filled with furniture found on the street, they often violated them in the most mundane of ways. They would show up to a job interview with a slightly too dark lipstick or with a well-used backpack instead of a leather shoulder bag or in tights that had a slightly too wide mesh so that they suggested fishnet stockings although they were not fishnet stockings or wearing a skirt that buttoned up the front and was just a little too short or one that had a slit that was a little too high even though not that high or wearing shoes that were just a little too thick-soled and urban. It was as if their unconscious had ingested all the rules of the dress code and then piled minor infraction on top of minor infraction so that no single item on its own would have noticeably violated the dress code but when all the clothing violations were assembled together they looked just a little off, a little suspect. They did not look rebellious, well dressed, aristocratic, intellectual, freethinking, transformative, or slightly sexy. They just looked off. They looked perhaps like they had just turned zombie, like they were one of those zombies that were not yet covered in rotten flesh with dirty, torn clothes, one of the zombies that humans might mistake for a few minutes as one of them and then a moment later, as they looked at them some more, it would dawn on the human that they were a zombie, a new zombie, and at the moment of this recognition the human would take a large board they had in their hand and hit them, the new zombie, across the face because humans hate zombies.

Their scholarly writing was similar. They insisted first on writing about those whom the complex considered to be minor literary figures. The complex considered these figures to be minor usually because these writers themselves often violated the rules in various small ways. So while they worked on writing that was often difficult, work that used fragmentation, quotation, disruption, disjunction, agrammatical syntax, and so on, in a profession that valued the difficult, they were partial to work that was syntactically difficult rather than work that was highly allusive. The complex preferred work that had conventional syntax and was full of weighty allusion. And then they refused on principle to present the writing of these minor figures as minor because they felt to do so was giving in to the values of the complex. And then they insisted on pretending as if this writing that valued fragmentation, quotation, disruption, disjunction, agrammatical syntax, and so on was only clear. They refused to acknowledge its tediums, its nonsense, its relentless obviousness. They acted as if all this writing had a great and evident value. And when they wrote about this work, they used the simplest language they could possibly use to talk about it rather than resorting to the highly theoretical language that was the most popular way to be a leftist or a rebel, the most popular way to show that they were rebellious, well dressed, aristocratic, intellectual, freethinking, transformative, or slightly sexy in the complex. It was like how they dressed. Just as their lipstick was a tad too dark, their skirt a tad too short, the soles of their shoes a tad too thick, their writing was a tad too obvious about works that had little obvious about them. At the same time, they refused to get rid of any of the awkward repetitions or the weird turns of phrase that they heard in their writing as musical but they knew those in the complex often heard as just weird and awkward.

For various reasons, these minor literary figures were writing work that mattered to them, work that they wanted to talk about with others. Whenever they had to express this in job interviews, when they were asked, in a voice most likely filled with concern or disdain or both, why they were interested in writing that used fragmentation, quotation, disruption, disjunction, agrammatical syntax, and so on, they wanted to dismiss the question by saying they liked to read it. But if they really wanted to answer this question they would have to tell a more personal story that would begin with the town they had grown up in, a small rural town in the middle of the continent, a town without libraries and bookstores, a town that was also ugly and dirty. The town was dirty because it had one industry, a paper mill. This meant it smelled very bad. The town was in a valley and so the smoke from the paper mill collected in the valley. When it snowed, the next day a layer of soot covered the ground. It was subtle, it wasn't like the things they say about the industrial revolution where things got so dirty that a certain sort of moth adapted by turning from a light color to a dark color, but it was there. When they complained about the smell and the soot in the town, other residents said that it sure smells like money to them. Behind that statement was the paper mill's threat that they could pick up and go down south at any moment if the smell stopped smelling like money and then the town would probably just disappear.

Because the town was dirty, whenever they read poems about the beauty of the countryside or the rich, dark woods of the eastern part of the continent or of the other continent and islands across the Atlantic, which was all they knew about poetry because the only poems they read in school were about stuff like this, poetry made little sense to them. So then they found this writing of fragmentation, quotation, disruption, disjunction, agrammatical syntax, and so on in an anthology. This writing was at the time over sixty years old and mainly written on the continent and the islands across the Atlantic and yet it felt completely fresh and new and because they were looking for something that was not a weird environmental lie, and because this writing of fragmentation, quotation, disruption, disjunction, agrammatical syntax, and so on was so weird it at least didn't seem to be lying in the usual ways and they clung to it and they felt it was a part of them.

Really what it was was that they felt this writing in their body. They felt certain sensations, the sensations of interested calmness that happened when their mind and their breath were working together. This sensation of interested calmness might also be called a pleasant boredom. There was something about the artfully vague repetition of this writing from afar that pleased them. It pleased them slightly but not too much and from this mild stimulation certain thoughts formed in their head and they felt they could pay attention to these thoughts and their emerging symbols as much or as little as they wanted.

Like their brain's interest in something as mundane as a kaleidoscope's colorful, changing patterns or the image of a drop of water falling and then the water below splashing up a little after the drop of water falls into the stillness of the standing water or the shifting patterns of traffic on a busy highway that are just similar enough to put them into a trance yet changing enough for them to remain alert, interested. When reading this work, they could relax into it and let it take over all the parts of their brain. For some reason they could not understand, writing that used fragmentation, quotation, disruption, disjunction, agrammatical syntax, and so on entered into their body and changed it.

And yet they did not give either of these answers when they were asked, in a voice most likely filled with concern or disdain or both, why they were interested in writing that used fragmentation, quotation, disruption, disjunction, agrammatical syntax, and so on. Instead they mumbled something about being interested in its indeterminancy or they would use some theoretical term in another language that was often used by the theorists of the seventies to describe an intimate and passionate feeling. They felt ashamed of this argument about being from a working-class family, from a small rural town in the middle of the continent, the town without libraries and bookstores, because it was not how being from a working-class family, from a small rural town in the middle of the continent, a town without libraries and bookstores, was supposed to work. Coming from a working-class family, from a small rural town in the middle of the continent, a town without libraries and bookstores, was supposed to make one interested in plain speech, in how deep thoughts might show up in the form of small aphorisms, in anecdotes about the weather which turned into anecdotes about how to live one's life. Or so the complex encouraged or perhaps trained them to think.

But still they kept going, going with job application after job application, writing article after article about this writing from afar that used fragmentation, quotation, disruption, disjunction, agrammatical syntax, and so on with a somewhat pious and not very well thought out sense of class politics. This somewhat pious and not very well thought out sense of class politics was mainly class emotion and little class reason. The complex taught them how to talk about being from a working-class family, from a small rural town in the middle of the continent, a town without libraries and bookstores, but once they began to talk about being from, it was clear to them that they were no longer of a working-class family, of a small rural town in the middle of the continent, a town without libraries and bookstores. The complex trained them to figure themselves as underprivileged, trained them to document their own past marginality, a marginality they had not felt until they left the working-class family, the small rural town in the middle of the continent, the town without libraries and bookstores, and were trained by the complex to notice their marginality. Before they had been trained by the complex to think of themselves as underprivileged, they saw themselves as privileged because they had access to so much because they had been born on a continent that was currently occupied by a very rich government. It was not that they did not see something like poverty around them. They saw a peculiar form of something like poverty that meant more than enough food but only a certain processed form of food, that meant television but not bookstores or libraries. But it was clear to them that in this small rural town in the middle of the continent, this town without libraries and bookstores, the residents of the town had more than enough food and water, and if they could not afford to buy it, the government would help them out. And not only that, they also had schooling and they had public parks and roads and some version of medical care. They did not at any moment think of themselves as marginal. When their high-school guidance counselor had told them that they could probably get a scholarship to a school for rich-kid slackers because they were from a rural industrialized region and schools for rich-kid slackers would see them as underprivileged, they were shocked.

Among all of them, only one of their parents had gone to college. One of their fathers, a father who had not gone to college, worshiped reading. As long as they were reading, their father did not make them do any chores. Reading, they would say, is more important. This caused them to be constantly reading in their childhood. And one of them had a mother who would say over and over that it did not matter what they read as a child, as long as they were reading. They grew to think of reading as a sort of magic talisman, a talisman that they could wear proudly on their lapel for all to see, a talisman that would let them be from but not of, from a working-class family, from a small rural town in the middle of the continent, a town without libraries and bookstores, but not of a working-class family, of a small rural town in the middle of the continent, a town without libraries and bookstores. Sort of how Frankenstein's creature had been from the monstrous but was no longer of the monstrous after they learned to read by looking through a peephole.

So they felt their lives changed by studying in the complex. They knew that going to the complex and paying their way in order to be a student in and of the complex was a way to learn how not to carry the signs of being from a working-class family, from a small rural town in the middle of the continent, a town without libraries and bookstores. And they were excellent students of this. Sometimes they stayed up all night studying this at the small private part of the complex for rich-kid slackers that they attended on a large scholarship after they left the small rural town in the middle of the continent, the town without libraries and bookstores. It was the complex that gave them the theoretical words from the seventies to describe their intimate relationship with the forms of writing that used fragmentation, quotation, disruption, disjunction, agrammatical syntax, and so on. But they did not just learn from the complex, they also learned from the culture that surrounded the complex. The rich-kid slackers had frequent parties and at the parties they discussed people like Andy Warhol, Carolee Schneeman, Robert Duncan, Jack Spicer, Patti Smith, Madonna, and Lou Reed. Most of these names they did not know so they made it a point to remember them and then they would go to the library the next day to try and figure out what these names represented. At the library, they spent most of their time not in the stacks with the books but in the periodical section reading various glossy magazines on art and music and the social scenes around art and music. They carried a notebook with them on these trips to the library and they would make a list of the names of various bands that were mentioned in the glossy magazines and then they would go back to their friends' dorm rooms and see if they had any albums by these bands that they would then borrow. They were grateful for the information about how not to carry the signs of being from a working-class family, from a small rural town in the middle of the continent, a town without libraries and bookstores, and so were their parents who were helping them pay the amounts of money in addition to the scholarship that the complex demanded from them to teach them how to be from but not of. They felt the complex open up their mind and they felt it place new things in the gray matter of their brain.

At the time they did not question their parents' devotion to the complex. They did not think that when their father gestured with their indirect and floppy gesture and said reading was more important than household chores that they might also be saying something untrue, something about how self-development was more important than the reciprocity of contributing to the household. They did not wonder if there was something wrong about participating in the complex that let some of their class enter the expansionism of the economy that currently occupied the continent on which they lived by paying money up front so as to get credentialed by the complex. They knew this father was obsessed with the complex because they had grown up in an orphanage that was on the outskirts of a private and very famous part of the complex that claimed to only educate the smartest but in reality educated a number of smart people but also educated the very rich and the descendents of those who had already attended the complex. They knew that their father who had not been able to attend the complex must have in those years felt there were two sorts of people, those alike and those unalike, those who wore a cloak of power, a cloak that was long and black and sometimes had black velvet stripes. They might have thought of these cloaks as emblazoned with an insignia in gold thread so as to bestow on those who had the right to wear them a certain light of connection, a sort of glowing orb of power that had tentacles and these tentacles reached out to others who wore cloaks and tentacles and when they met, two wearers of these cloaks and tentacles, their tentacles would intertwine in pleasure.

But when it came down to it, they had to admit their class politics did not hold up all that well. They saw the complex's problems and felt these problems as a restrictive steel band around their chest, a band that prevented them from doing the work they wanted to do in the way they wanted to do it. And yet they also had to admit that they were the ones who tightened this band every night before they went to bed. They looked around them and they could see how the complex welcomed those who were more in control of their unconscious resistance or were perhaps even conscious of their resistance. The complex prided itself on its external diversity even as it demanded allegiance to its rules and so it liked to point to those from a working-class family, from a small rural town in the middle of the continent, a town without libraries and bookstores, within it as evidence of its inclusive politics. The complex did not even demand that they give up the parts of themselves that were characteristic of being from a working-class family, from a small rural town in the middle of the continent, a town without libraries and bookstores. It would let them keep their way of saying can't as cain't, of saying wash as warsh, of saying crayon as crown. It would let them say riceling for riesling and find it a cute sign of how they were from a working-class family, from a small rural town in the middle of the continent, a town without libraries and bookstores. It would let them talk righteously about their fathers who had not gone through the complex and their blue-collar jobs and with this righteousness it would tell a story of itself as inclusive. And they let this happen, they signed an agreement to let the complex use them in this way when they went to a bank and signed for a loan to cover the tuition that remained after the scholarship because they longed to be a part of the complex and they wanted to no longer be of a small rural town in the middle of the continent, a town without libraries and bookstores. They wanted instead to easily pay the bills and to watch films from other places and to have political discussions late at night in bars full of all different sorts of people and to regularly eat foods full of spices, foods prepared in a wide variety of ways that had their roots in many different cultures and parts of the world.

When they moved to the island in the middle of the Pacific they moved because of a job at a part of the complex that was not one of those first established on the continent. It was a decent job, it paid more than enough money to eat the unsustainable amounts of protein that they and people like them ate and to consume the unsustainable amount of fossil fuels that they and people like them consumed, but it was not a very prestigious job by the standards of the complex. And because they assumed the standards of the complex and because they had a somewhat pious and not very well thought out sense of class politics and because they thought of themselves as a zombie, they thought of themselves as an outsider starting a job in a minor part of the complex, but not in the real heart of the complex. They felt that because the job was just a decent job but not a prestigious job, that they still were not emotionally part of the complex and even more, they felt that the complex knew this and that this was obvious to people both inside and outside the complex. It was like their relationship to the government that currently occupied the continent and fossil fuels and wars. No one ever asked them if it was fine to use so much fossil fuel and kill so many people and if asked they would answer no and not only that, they would willingly give up all the things that come with fossil fuels and wars. Even more, they felt that the government that currently occupied the continent knew this, knew they would answer no, and that this was obvious to many people. Similarly, they felt they were not really an active part of the complex. They felt that the complex had only let them in because they had repeatedly beaten their head against the door until they found a moment of weakness and then when the door finally gave they had slipped in. But they also suspected that it might not last, the way they were inside the complex, that they might at any moment be found out and shown the door. Especially since, now that they were in, they were somewhat dizzy from bashing their head against the door and their brain was a little addled and their work was suffering as a result although they continued writing articles and giving talks with a zombielike regularity. Their feeling about their status as a zombie was so intense and persuasive to themselves that when they read descriptions of the emotions of alienation and that weird combination of attraction and revulsion that so defined alienation, they felt as if they were talking to them or maybe even about them. Like when they read works by the colonized about their attraction or their revulsion at the same moment towards colonial cultures they thought to themselves that this was how they felt towards the complex. Or they thought of their relationship to the complex when they heard their friend from afar, from a small island nation in the Pacific with a long history of occupation by other nations, describe the emotion han, an emotion that combines sadness with hope, as the emotion that happens as a result of repeated colonization. They were smart enough not to indulge in a self-satisfied feeling of being marginal; neither did they think there was a one-to-one equation between something like han and their zombie feeling. They recognized the structural differences, the differences that matter. They knew that to compare their relationship to the educational complex with colonization was a funny, perhaps even amoral, comparison. And they also recognized their own political ineffectiveness, the way they were as much a part of the problem as anything else and that this sort of thinking was risky because it might allow them to concentrate on their emotions and ignore their structural role in the colonization. But still on a personal level, they felt something. When they read a colonized intellectual writing about how the colonized live under the sign of a contradiction that loomed at every step and deprived them of all coherence and tranquility, they felt emotions. And they felt it also when they read how the colonized lived under the mark of the plural, drowned in an anonymous collectivity that takes over their ability to talk about themselves as anything other than they. And they liked to think of these emotions as the beginning of a politics of some sort, as the baby steps that would move them to action.

But when they got to the island they realized that they were something different, they were not the zombie who had fooled everyone and slipped in. They were of the complex, a complex that was set up for them and by them. They were the haole schoolteacher, a figure that shows up in numerous poems and novels written on the island. As the haole schoolteacher, they suddenly were someone who had a series of arbitrary rules that must be followed to the letter. They were committed to their way of grammar and spelling, so committed that they beat or otherwise humiliated students who did not follow their rules. They allowed only a certain number of bathroom breaks, no matter the needs of the students' bladders. They gave out wrong information and punished students for not reciting it back incorrectly. They told histories where colonizers were liberators. They were devoted to literacy and argued that civilization was impossible without it. They made students wear itchy and too tight shoes that pinched. And they were always improperly dressed, perhaps wearing slips and panty hose beneath their skirts, items that were wrong for the climate and then they were, as a result, sweating a little too much and thus had a slightly stale smell. They were always too red in the face, a red face caused not only by sun on their fair skin and improper, overly warm, dress but also by frustration, the frustration that happens when they are in a foreign culture and cannot figure out the rules and thus get angry and flustered. This emotion caused a certain rigidity in their body, a strange way of walking and even created a strange way of thinking. The haole school teacher in the poems and novels was someone who made students write imitations of Wordsworth's poem Daffodils despite the fact that daffodils could never grow in the tropics. But mainly and most horrifically, they were mediocre. And the reasoning was this: if they were not mediocre, they would not be teaching on an island in the middle of the Pacific, they would be teaching on the continent.

So once they got to the island in the middle of the Pacific, they realized that the complex did not just provide training in how to act as if one was not from working-class families from small rural towns in the middle of the continent, towns without libraries and bookstores. It was more complicated than that. It was a hugely successful part of colonialism. The version of the complex that had been set up on the island in the middle of the Pacific clearly reflected the values and concerns of those who arrived from afar. Of all the institutions on the island it had done the least mixing, the least of that constant even if often unequal exchange that so defined life on the island and produced things like the particular creole that those who were born on the island spoke and a special way of tuning a guitar so that it had many different chords but usually had a major chord, or a chord with a major seventh note or sometimes with a sixth note in it. They had to instead think of the complex as a very powerful institution designed for the most mundane sorts of socialization to western values. And then they had to think about their own presence and role in this complex and this socialization.

They taught in a department whose purpose was to teach the literature that was written in a language that had a long colonial history, an expansionist language that was spreading to more and more places every day. The resonances of this expansion were especially felt in their time, when more and more languages were disappearing every day, disappearing so quickly that some predicted that at least 90 percent of the languages in the world would disappear in the next hundred years. This department offered many courses in the many centuries of the literature written on an island in the Atlantic where the expansionist language originated, and many courses in the last two centuries of literature written on the nearest continent that was occupied by the same government that now occupied the island in middle of the Pacific, a few courses in literature written on the islands right now, and no courses in the literature written on the island before the arrival of the whaling ships. And it was not that the department of the expansionist language was especially conservative. It was not. It was at the time attempting to be attentive to the issues that many who had genealogical ties to the island from before the whaling ships arrived raised. It was seen by some as dogmatically leftist and by others as politically engaged. But the local branch of the complex was structured so that even if the department of the expansionist language wanted to change, it was constantly thwarted. Not only by its internal fights, which were many and intense as it attempted to be more responsible to some of the issues raised by some of those who had genealogical ties to the island from before the whaling ships arrived, but mainly by the complex itself. Written into the charter of the local branch of the complex was a statement that its purpose was to educate the immigrants who arrived to this island, a statement that deliberately ignored the presence of the people who were there before the whaling ships arrived. As a result, it was hard to get the version of the complex on the island in the middle of the Pacific to recognize the need to be attentive to the culture that had been on the island before the whaling ships arrived. So when the department of the expansionist language finally stopped fighting about whether to hire someone who wrote and studied the literature written by those who had genealogical ties to the island from before the whaling ships arrived and decided it was a good idea to do this, it was caught by the complex's policies that felt a local branch of the complex should not hire its own graduates and yet the only place to study the literature of those who had genealogical ties to the island from before the whaling ships arrived was at the local branch of the complex on the island.

They thought of the complex, both the part of it on the island in the middle of the Pacific and the whole thing, as a giant octopus. It had a soft body and a well-developed brain. The complex, like the octopus, tended to dig its own den and then close the entrance with stones. The complex tended to seize its prey with its eight long arms, arms with suckers on them and with these suckers, there were hundreds of them, the complex could hold onto almost anything. The complex sucked the flesh of various crustaceans and discarded the empty shells. If the complex lost one of its tentacles, it would soon grow another one in the same place. Along with its eight arms and hundreds of suckers, the complex had an eye on each side of its head. While the complex had very keen eyesight, it was also completely deaf. And when it was attacked, the complex could shoot a smokescreen of black ink at its attackers that allowed the complex time to escape if it needed. The complex could also camouflage itself by changing its skin color or texture so that it matched its surroundings. It could squeeze through the tiniest hole, move around on its arms, and scoot backwards rapidly by shooting a jet of water through its body.

They knew within a few months of arriving on the island that they had been wrong about being a zombie. They were in no way a zombie. They were instead one of the suckers on one of the complex's tentacles. They realized the whole idea that they could actually be zombies was hopelessly romantic, despite all the unromantic rotting flesh. They were something smaller than zombies. They were suckers. They were not even in the shape of the human, they were instead one small ring of circular and meridional muscles surrounded by supple sheets of connective tissue and epithelia among many attached to one of eight arms of an octopus. And when they grappled and clasped at things they did it not on their own but with others around them. They were one sucker among many on one of eight arms. And when one of the tentacles flailed about they flailed about with it. When one of the suckers on the tentacles who was from afar flailed about and demanded the resignation of a professor who had genealogical ties to the island from before the whaling ships arrived because they were outspoken, they were a part of that demand even if they did not sign the letter that demanded the resignation. When students urged faculty to keep an other than the expansionist language requirement and institute an ethnic studies requirement and one of the suckers on the tentacles from afar flailed around and began heckling the students by unzipping their pants and saying to the students do you want to fuck with me?; let's fuck, they too were unzipping their pants and saying do you want to fuck with me?; let's fuck. When one of suckers on the tentacle from afar said that the culture that was on the islands from before the whaling ships arrived did not have a literature because they could not write until after the whaling ships arrived and so they shouldn't bother teaching any courses in that literature, they too were a part of that. It was impossible for them to act independently.

Once they realized that they were just a sucker on one tentacle of the complex, the teaching issue was even more complicated. When teaching, they soon realized, they were essentially recruiting people to recognize the expansionist language and literature as the right language and literature for the island. Further, they had arrived on the island with a detailed and nuanced understanding of what they suddenly realized was only a small section of the literature from afar. They knew a lot about forms of writing that used fragmentation, quotation, disruption, disjunction, agrammatical syntax, and so on that was written either on the continent and island across the Atlantic or on the continent across the Pacific but not that much about writing that used fragmentation, quotation, disruption, disjunction, agrammatical syntax, and so on that was from other places. And they knew almost nothing about writing that used timeline-based narrative structures from any place. They could talk at great length about how this literature that used fragmentation, quotation, disruption, disjunction, agrammatical syntax, and so on resists or revolts. But usually when they said these words they meant that the literature resists or revolts against certain literary norms and conventions, not against large political structures like colonialism.

They had learned to use the words resistance and revolution and to really mean only resistance and revolution against literary genres in graduate school. They had gone to graduate school in a cold place that was known for its study of the radical and saw itself as outsider. There was lots of attention to the techniques of formally radical literature and the legacies of this literature. As graduate students they had met weeknights in various bars and cafes that served alcohol late at night, after they had done some reading and some writing alone in their large yet cold rented apartments, and talked about things. They braved the cold and the ice to talk about things. The things they talked about were things like radical modernism. And legacies. And male poets. They talked not reflectively about male poets as male poets, but compulsively about male poets as if they were not even noticing that they just talked about male poets. They could not help themselves. There was a heroic tendency in the cold place that felt as if it were a warm breeze. A heroism that came from dealing with the cold and snow more than most other places. A heroism that came from a city dealing with a steel industry now gone and the reminder of a once thriving machismo that was now at risk. And a heroism that came from a city dealing with repeated and absurd losses in various superbowls. A heroism of a city of numerous bars and cafes that served alcohol. The discussion they had late at night in those warm bars was often about the radicalness of something written. A work that was radical was a good work. At the time it was difficult to describe what being radical meant. It meant more a feeling, a hard-to-read feeling. Or something they were not used to reading. It meant maybe ellipitical they thought. Or they learned to define it as basically any literature that was good at educating how not to bear the signs of being from working-class families, from small rural towns in the middle of the continent, towns without libraries and bookstores. Eventually they would define what they had meant by radical as writing that used modernist techniques of fragmentation, quotation, disruption, disjunction, agrammatical syntax, and so on. A work that was radical used more modernist techniques than other works. It was not all that simple, they had to admit. Content did matter at the time. But often as an afterthought. And even if the question of radical enough was not stated bluntly it was often implied or lurking behind another question, such as: was the work any good? Radical enough was also a game that men won more than women, although there was a certain woman modernist who always won all aspects of the game if they were brought in. Yet somehow that did not seem much of a comfort.

In graduate school they had been taught a map of poetry that had the avant-garde squaring off at the borders against various national literary conventions. But when they got to the island in the middle of the Pacific and looked at the poetry that surrounded them they realized that this map of poetry that they had been taught in graduate school no longer made sense and they had to make new maps. Their old map had only one line, a horizontal line, and they placed the avant-garde's use of fragmentation, quotation, disruption, disjunction, agrammatical syntax, and so on on one side and on the other side they placed the national literature's conventional language use. But once they looked at the literature around them on the island in the middle of the Pacific, they had to add a vertical line. So they added a vertical axis and on one side they placed community exploration and the other side self-exploration. So now they divided literary conventions into four. In the upper left, community exploration and fragmentation, quotation, disruption, disjunction, agrammatical syntax, and so on; in the upper right, self exploration and fragmentation, quotation, disruption, disjunction, agrammatical syntax, and so on; in the lower left, community exploration and national literature's conventional language use; in the lower right, self-exploration and national literature's conventional language use. And they made charts where they put various poets and poetry schools in these various boxes. They knew this was not enough but they felt it was a beginning at least.

Trying to figure out where to place things in this new map, they looked at the poetry around them. They looked in particular at the poetry written by those who had genealogical ties to the island from before the whaling ships arrived. It slowly dawned on them, but it was so obvious that they could not understand how they had managed to not think on it before, that poetry had a different resonance, a different importance in places of activist anticolonialism. All sorts of poetry. Both radical and not so radical. Both poems written in the expansionist language and poems written in the language that had been on the island before the whaling ships arrived and poems written in the pidgins and creoles, the burrowing languages, the negotiated languages. Many people involved in various political movements on the island were also poets. Poems were read at protests with great regularity. The genre's assumed shortness, its lack of rules and structures, and its links to orality made it a genre of populist protest. This poetry used all sorts of different tools. It used tools from the continent and tools from other islands. It used fragmentation, quotation, disruption, disjunction, agrammatical syntax, and so on. It used confession and epiphany. It used localism and internationalism. It used insult and anger. It used sentiment. No matter what, poetry used all these tools for an anticolonial message. It was so extreme that they guessed that 70 to 80 percent of all the published poetry written by those who had genealogical ties to the island from before the whaling ships arrived was at this time anticolonial in content and written so as to educate or provoke others to action around sovereignty issues. And yet they could say almost nothing consistent about how the poems were formed. It was not that this poetry was innocent. It, like all poetries, had its problems, its biases, its narrownesses, its just plain badnesses. But it was still uniquely driven by community concerns and assumed activist readers of poetry.

It had taken them so long to see this because when they looked at poetry they tended to look at how it was made, not what it made, not its resonances in the world. But suddenly seeing the waves that resonated out of poetry on the island focused their vision. Where before they had seen amateurish chaos and a lack of formal allegiance, they now saw a concentrated effort to try all the tools in order to achieve a singular goal. They had been looking, they realized, through the wrong end of the telescope and now, once they had learned to look through the end with the eyepiece, they were able to focus in and see.

Further, the poetry that was attentive to the sovereignty movement on this island in the middle of the Pacific demanded not only that they see their writing and their teaching position as carrying expansionist histories and thus responsibility, but it also redefined the questions. It was like the radical issue. It was not that they had to give up seeing the radical in terms of modernist techniques. It was that they had to see the radical in a new way, just as they had come to use the term continent rather than mainland or as they had come to see the expanses of ocean as connection rather than disconnection. They began to see poetry as a series of contiguous systems, systems that did not merge but that were still beside one another. They found themselves asking who they wrote with and why. They found themselves questioning ambiguity and its presumed neutrality in their work. They brought these questions into their classroom messily. They paused and stuttered a lot. They contradicted themselves and they got confused. They are not heroes in this story. But they did learn some things and begin thinking differently by looking at the poetries around them. They learned through muddling and they trudged through these issues with others.

They had been hired to teach the literature written in the expansionist language at the local branch of the complex. But they were poets so they had an uneasy role in the standoff in the department between those who taught how to read the literature of the expansionist language and those who taught how to write the literature of the expansionist language. This was an old fight and it was a fight that was imported from the continent. In this fight, various sides accused each other of various things that were not really true in any nuanced sense. Those who taught how to write the literature of the expansionist language accused those who taught how to read the literature of the expansionist language of only looking at various political and economic influences and thus not understanding the beauty of literature because to them it was just politics, or even more specifically, just identity politics. While those who taught how to read the literature of the expansionist language felt that those who taught how to write the literature of the expansionist language were politically retrograde because all they did was talk about literary traditions and various details and nuances of craft. While they knew that the truth was somewhere between these two positions, they had to admit that they were troubled with how creative writing was taught. Creative writing departments, whether on the island or on the continent, rarely addressed what it might mean to be training people to write only in the expansionist language and to assign as examples almost exclusively writing written in the expansionist language. Further it was no coincidence that the huge growth in creative writing departments that began in the late seventies and early eighties, a growth that the program at the local branch of the complex was a part of, happened at the exact same moment as the rise of community poetries. The complex's program in creative writing on the island was created at the same time that two parallel literary and cultural renaissances happened in the community, a cultural and political renaissance by those who had genealogical ties to the island from before the whaling ships arrived and a literary renaissance by those who were born on the island but whose parents or grandparents came from afar and who wrote in the creole that people spoke as they sat around talking, drinking beers, and eating plates of meat and rice on their lanais at night. So as more and more communities took back poetry, the creative writing program of the local branch of the complex tried to pretend more and more as if the complex still owned poetry as it had in the middle of the century.

This issue about who should teach how to write literature was complicated by a friend who like them came from afar and who refused to teach creative writing even though they had published several novels because they felt that creative writing is so tied to the community that it should only be taught by those who had genealogical ties to the island from before the whaling ships arrived. They were lost in this argument for some time. Was it better to refuse to teach creative writing and thus leave it to those who were already teaching in an unexamined, most likely even unconscious, way that denigrated the concerns of community poetries? Or was it better to take up space as a sort of ally from afar and from that space insist that more space be made for those writers who had genealogical ties to the island from before the whaling ships arrived? Whatever the answer, it was obvious that the institution had a tendency to refuse change. Those in control of creative writing at the local branch of the complex on the island in the Pacific acted as if their values were neutral and innocent yet they were not at all innocent when it came to defending them. When some on the faculty suggested that the department should hire a writer who wrote in one of the local languages, one of the languages created by the arrival of the expansionist language, the pidgins and creoles, the burrowing languages, the negotiated languages, others on the faculty were so upset that they insisted this position, which had been called the Visiting Distinguished Writer, now be called the Visiting Writer because one could not really be distinguished if one was writing in one of the local languages. When other departments, such as the department for the study of the culture and the language that was on the island before the whaling ships arrived, wanted to teach creative writing and literature because they saw literature as part of their political and cultural renaissance, some on the faculty voted against allowing courses like this to be a part of the expansionist language major. When yet another distinguished visiting writer was hired and they wanted to teach a writing workshop about how to write in the languages that were formed by the arrival of the expansionist language, the pidgins and creoles, the burrowing languages, the negotiated languages, some faculty told their students not to take it, especially their students from the continent because they said that these students would have nothing to learn from a writing workshop about writing in the languages that were created by the arrival of the expansionist language, the pidgins and creoles, the burrowing languages, the negotiated languages. In this way the creative writing department attempted to build a bunker.

Yet the bunker could not hold. It could not hold because the people who came to study creative writing at the local branch of the complex often brought their community poetries with them and refused to give them up when they got to the local branch of the complex. And then once there they began to agitate to change the local branch of the complex. For instance, the workshop in the local languages, the languages that were created by the arrival of the expansionist language, the pidgins and creoles, the burrowing languages, the negotiated languages was fully enrolled when it was eventually offered and it even had a number of students from the continent in it. So they felt optimistic at times because creative writing was a fairly new institution and it might still be a place where poetries of community activism were acknowledged, strengthened, challenged. A place where poetry, in the words of a poet activist who had genealogical ties to the island from before the whaling ships arrived, was seen as decolonization and re-creation; as a place for exposé and celebration; as a furious but nurturing aloha. Their optimism was small and tempered. And yet it was there.

That vague optimism was something about the island in the middle of the Pacific that was hard to explain, yet it was a story they could tell over and over. It was the story of the land snails that might have arrived to the island by a prehistoric chain of steppingstone islands. And the story of the honeycreepers—the ʻiʻiwi and the ʻapapane and the ʻākohekohe—who lived on the island before humans arrived yet no one knew how they got there because the birds were incapable of flying between islands. And the koa with its wide, expansive canopy and the koa's nearest relative over five thousand miles away. And the hurricane winds that carry spores, seeds, and insects. And the migratory paths of the ruddy turnstone, the wandering tattlers, the sanderling, the pintail duck, and the shoveler duck. And the video of the man walking on the atoll that was no longer an atoll because it was under water.

This tiny optimism developed into a flipping back and forth between love and confusion, acceptance and alienation, fascination and anger. It was a series of zeros and ones that could be put together to make something buggy but executable. And the more time they spent in the Pacific, the more intensely they thought about these various emotions even as they grew more and more accepting of the parts of the island that induced negative emotions. They grew accustomed to spending their days moving through a series of extreme emotions about the place where they lived. One moment they would think about the luminous beauty of the island: the spinelike pattern of reds and greens and yellows in the croton's leaf or the kukui clustered in veinlike streams down the crevice of a ravine because kukui grows in places that are moist or they would thrill to something that was only available on the island, some plant like the silversword that had developed from the Pacific coast tarweed into something long, silver-protruding, and covered with balls or they would enjoy some word or concept that was only in the language of the place that was there before the language that they had learned from birth had come to the place and brought with it a series of oppressions and assumptions. And then the next moment would come along and they would find that they could think only with guilt, guilt for living on the islands and their inevitable alliance to the dominant would overtake them. Their stomachs would sink whenever anyone complained about those damn haoles and their institutions of development, anthropology, or haolewood. It would sink because they agreed. Because they recognized the problems with these institutions. And because they also realized how the institutions were a part of them, how they shaped them and how they surrounded them and how they supported these institutions just by being the sort of person that the institutions supported even as they wanted to move out and away from this institutional and unwanted cloud and into the warm sun of the Pacific.

Eventually, they began to feel comfortable with the emotions and the cloud, began to see these things as normal, as part of the way people thought when they acknowledged the history of any place in which they lived. And they felt their thoughts gave their lives something incalculable and indescribable, not a richness but some sort of loud, brash coloring that they became fond of and no longer saw as loud and brash but instead saw as soothing and comforting. They recognized the specificity of their thoughts and this helped them to understand that their thoughts were of this time, this moment. And how in the history of the human, they were short-term and historically and politically specific thoughts. And if they wanted they could rise up out of the thoughts and float over the history of the place and see their thoughts as a small dot on the timeline of thoughts and realize that the moment in which they lived was just a small part of history. When they rose up out of the moment and floated it didn't make these thoughts any less valid, but it explained how these thoughts were something they had to deal with if they wanted to float back down and be living in the now. And they wanted this. They wanted to live in now.

5

But still, despite the measured, tiny optimism, or perhaps because of it, this issue of where they should be on the bus, in the room, on the globe, this issue of belonging, felt often like it hit them in the gut, by which they meant it hit them where it mattered, it hit them in their bodies and, in their bodies, it hit them specifically in the palm of their writing hand, in that space that their little and ring fingers made when they held a pen, the space that when they were learning to write in first grade they had been forced to fill with a small cool marble so as to learn the proper way of holding a pencil. There was so much discussion and so much talk around writing on the island. So much pressure. Some of it productive. Some of it not. The pressure was unfortunately all inclusive. Everybody got pressure from somebody. Those born on the island but whose parents or grandparents were from afar got it. And those with genealogical ties to islands other than this island in the Pacific from before the whaling ships arrived got it. And those who had genealogical ties to the island from before the whaling ships arrived but who were born on the continent and who maybe or maybe not came back to the island later in life got it. And those who had genealogical ties and were born on the island but moved away from the island got it. And those who had genealogical ties and were born on the island and lived on the island got it. The pressure was not evenly distributed. Some got more pressure than others. And the content of the pressure varied. But in most instances, the birthplace of their parents or grandparents or great-grandparents or great-great-grandparents or great-great-great-grandparents determined the sort of pressure.

Eventually, they decided to let both the absurdities and the productive tensions around these historical ways of categorizing people that were imposed on everyone by imperialism be a starting point. They began making elaborate charts to try to figure out this issue of where they should be on the bus, in the room, on the globe, this issue of belonging that felt as if it hit them in the palm of their writing hand. The chart that they attempted to construct categorized the options for writers who like them had arrived from afar. The chart would begin with two categories: writers from afar who dealt with the island in their writing and writers from afar who did not. Then each of these two categories could be further broken into two other categories. The writers from afar who did not deal with the island category would become split into writers from afar who did not deal with the island in their work because they thought the island and its culture were small and uninteresting and writers from afar who did not deal with the island in their work because they felt that anything they might say as someone who came from afar would just be further cultural appropriation. So in other words the category of not dealing with the island in their writing would become split into those who did this out of disregard and those who did this out of respect. Similarly, among those who were from afar and who dealt with the island in their writing, there would also be two other subcategories: those from afar who felt they could just deal with the island because they were there, that when they moved to the island from afar they gained the right to talk about it, and those from afar who felt they had no right but rather the responsible thing to do in their writing was to talk about the island, especially to write about how the island was colonized in order to keep stating this thing because it was not necessarily acknowledged by everyone everywhere. This last subcategory of those who felt that they had a responsibility to write about how the island was colonized in their writing and yet also had to constantly position themselves as not from the island often wrote things that were endlessly, almost absurdly, self-reflective. They themselves were in this last category. But they did not think that their position on this chart was necessarily the correct position. If they knew anything at all, they knew they could never fully avoid the many problems of being a writer from afar in a place so colonized. But they also felt that they had to act as if it might be possible to write something that was not the wrong thing because to not act as if this might be possible was to risk being even more a part of the problem. They did not want to be like those who had a dismissive lack of interest in the island nor like those who were filled with anger at the island because the island induced in them funny feelings of being out of place and strange or made them think about things they would rather not think about such as how they were colonizers.

On top of all this anxiety, they added more. They also knew that they were not only writers from afar, but they were writers who wrote in the expansionist language. They themselves knew this expansionist language as their first language because of its expansionism. They had learned this language from birth and their parents had learned it from birth, but their grandparents had learned other languages at birth and came later to the expansionist language, except for one grandmother who had learned the expansionist language because the island on which they had been born had been coerced to give up its language first by settlers from a nation that spoke the expansionist language and then later by a school system that punished those who did not speak the expansionist language.

On the island in the middle of the Pacific, this expansionist language had arrived on the whaling ships. Many of the people who lived on the island, not only those from afar but also those born on the island but with parents or grandparents from afar and also those with genealogical ties to the island from before the whaling ships arrived, spoke this language. Many people told one another that they loved one another in this language. And many wrote their grocery lists in this language. And many called out to one another in this language when they saw one another on the street and got angry and screamed out their anger with one another in this language. And when they worked fifteen-hour days in the service industry they worked most often in this language. And even when they chatted with one another in a creole as they sat around talking, drinking beers, and eating plates of meat and rice on their lanais at night, the creole they spoke, while it was undeniably its own language, was very close to this expansionist language. They did this even though there had been a perfectly good language on the island for many years before the whaling ships arrived, a language that most human ears heard as unusually beautiful.

Some called the expansionist language a cultural bomb. And they could see all the ways this might be true on the island. The expansionist language was so good at expansion that it often absorbed in order to kill out the local languages. And it also slowly expanded over the languages that were often created by its arrival, the pidgins and creoles, the burrowing languages, the negotiated languages. For instance, the creole that many people born on the island spoke when talking to other people also born on the island was so close to this expansionist language because the expansionist language was slowly taking over the mix of different languages that had originally formed the creole. The expansionist language expanded regularly and steadily. This expansion was not innocent. The expansionist language had become the language that most people spoke not because it was more beautiful and not because it was easier and not because it had more literature but because of a law that from 1896 to 1970 had banned the language that had been spoken on the island for many years before the whaling ships arrived. But the expansionist language continued to expand so well not only because of these laws, but also because of the legacies of imperialism: the coercive economic dominance of the governments who spoke the expansionist language, the military might of the governments who spoke the expansionist language, and the technology industry and its alliances with the entertainment industry.

And yet, despite the expansionist language and all its tools, all the laws and all the imperialism, all the economic dominance, all the military might, all the technologies, and all the entertainments, the language politics of the island remained endlessly complicated. The expansion did not happen overnight and one could point to how the local languages and the languages that were often created by the arrival of the expansionist language to someplace new, the pidgins and creoles, the burrowing languages, the negotiated languages, refused to go away as evidence of how the expansionist language might not be as good at expansion as one might think. Undeniably, the expansion took some time, some generations. It was often contested. Often it would expand and manage almost to kill a local language and then the local language would rise up again and reassert itself. But despite the resurgence of the local languages on the island, the expansionist language continued to expand and at best it brokered an uneasy peace with the local language and allowed the local language to exist beside it, claiming the business of the technology industry and the entertainment industry for itself and yet allowing some songs to be sung and some poems and stories to be written in either or both the local language and the languages that were often created by the arrival of the expansionist language, the pidgins and creoles, the burrowing languages, the negotiated languages; on the island, it even allowed a few classes to be taught in the local language.

They knew that the problem with the expansionist language was not just that it could be a cultural bomb. It was not just the expansionist language that was the problem. After all, culture happened even in the expansionist language. They themselves were fine with how the language they had learned from birth was the expansionist language even though they had no genealogical ties to the people who had felt that this language was their own. They had not wished that their lullabies were in another, truer language when they were a child. They had never felt that they could not love their mothers or each other enough because the various names by which they called their mothers and each other were in the expansionist language. And if they looked at the histories of any location they saw poems and songs thriving and surviving any change of language. The culture might change, the poems and songs might rhyme differently or form different patterns to better meet the sounds of the language, but no matter what, any language was fully capable of expressing the special emotions that tended to come with having to negotiate an oppressive and foreign government on one's own land, an intense anger towards those from afar combined with a love of those near, plus a love of the land and a love of the things on the land, a love say of how the kukui clustered in veinlike streams down the crevice of a ravine, a love of heart-shaped velvety leaves that undulated from graceful stalks in a soft breeze, a love of the varieties of squeaks, whistles, rasping notes, and clicking sounds of the 'i'iwi. But they understood still how this did not mean that they wanted someone to come from afar and make them train their children in a language from afar so that their children would whisper in their lovers' ears in a language that was the language of those from afar. They understood that no one wanted this. They knew that people felt cultural loss in different ways and for different reasons. And that their not feeling loss might have a lot to do with their feeling that most of their grandparents had chosen to move to this place where the expansionist language was spoken and then had chosen to speak the language not because anyone made them with laws or with guns but because they wanted to, because they recognized the financial rewards of doing so, rewards that they themselves now reaped two generations later. And they also were concerned that with the loss of all the different sorts of languages, with the loss of the pidgins and the creoles, with the loss of the burrowing languages, with the loss of the negotiated languages, with the loss of the resistant languages, with the loss of the local languages that refused travel or were not interested in travel came the loss of specific and unique and stunningly beautiful and meaningful local information. Not only were certain specific cultural traditions lost, but particular, deep, and specific information such as the many names of the winds or the characteristics of the over three hundred different varieties of kalo were lost. The expansionist language did not have the vocabulary that let it carry this information. There was no way that the expansionist language could carry all the local knowledge because the expansionist language was only able to be expansionist because it claimed to be universal, neutral, objective, because it did not name the winds so specifically.

Nor was it that the local languages and the languages that were often created by the arrival of the expansionist language to some place new, the pidgins and creoles, the burrowing languages, the negotiated languages, were necessarily libratory. Or that language was innocent. Or that if they just switched languages they would be free of their anxieties. Yet despite this, they realized that when they wrote their poems, their essays, their software programs, even their grocery lists in the expansionist language, they immediately became not only a part of the expansionism by the accident of birth but they became willful agents of expansionism. When they wrote, they wrote as war machine. When they wrote, they wrote as ideological state apparatus. When they wrote, they wrote as military-industrial complex. This list went on and on. They wrote as colonial educational system. They wrote as the bulldozing of the land and the building of unnecessary roads. They wrote as the filling in of wetlands with imported sand to build beaches. And they wrote as the ever-expanding tourist industry. And while all of them were well schooled in the avant-garde, an avant-garde that used fragmentation, quotation, disruption, disjunction, agrammatical syntax, and so on to make them like a foreigner in their own language, they were finally not all that sure that using fragmentation, quotation, disruption, disjunction, agrammatical syntax, and so on escaped any of the expansionism. They wanted to believe the avant-garde claim that they could write so as to move between the borders of languages, that they could write beyond the ease of metaphors if they kept piling them up, one on top of another, that they could write from third spaces, that they could write so as to abolish colonialism if they did not use narrative continuity. And yet they also felt that this was somewhat absurd.

This issue of the expansionist language was not the only pressure on writing. There was also the risk of appropriation, another sort of cultural bomb. It was clear to them that there was such a long tradition of appropriation that anything they might say they would have to say sideways, have to say by doing more burrowing, negotiating, resisting, localizing, and refusing. One unfortunate result of the infection that they had was that it was hard for them to see anything with any nuance. They saw their options only as the one or the other. The island had played a large role in the literary and filmic imaginaries of the culture that currently occupied the continent that now claimed the island. In this imaginary, the island was a welcoming multicultural paradise filled with beautiful young women and wise old people who did not ask for much and shared their land and food and culture and even welcomed their colonizers as civilizers. These were stories the colonizers told to tell how they were welcomed. They did not want to write things like this. But the other response that they saw when they looked around them, the response of some who were like them from afar, was to ignore the island and build a bunker. This did not feel right either. It was clear that there were no easy answers to any of this and it was also clear that more than one answer was probably necessary. Yet whenever another one presented itself, they tended to distrust it and so they were caught rejecting every answer and thus never able to accumulate more than one answer.

At moments all this one or the other made them feel optimistic and excited. There was something about negotiating between various dualities and oppositions that was if not liberating, at least massively instructive. It was like the sun in this place. The sun was bright and stimulating. It was an antioxidant and produced melanin in their skin that in turn blocked ultraviolet rays. It felt good to be out in the sun and they liked to feel the sun heating up their skin, feel its stimulation, feel it causing some sort of chemical reaction that relaxed their muscles, their brain, and then filled them with small feelings of mild euphoria. And their feeling that they might some day figure things out if they kept thinking about things with generosity and an open mind and heart was to them an antioxidant and a protectant and yet another small feeling of mild euphoria. But they also knew that because they were from afar and because their relatives were from afar they could not stay too long in the sun thinking and trying to figure things out no matter if they did it with generosity or if they did it with anger as the rays would injure their blood vessels and swelling and reddening would result.

One thing was clear: those writers who like them arrived from the continent and even those who had been born on the island but had relatives who arrived after the whaling ships arrived dealt with this sun in different ways. They had different positions and they thought things out differently. Even in their house they had different positions on the chart. One of them was in the last category, the category of writers from afar who wrote about the island and then the subcategory of those who felt that they had a responsibility to write about how the island was colonized in their writing, and one of them was in the category of those who did not write about the island because they were not interested in it, and one of them was in the category of those who did not write about the island because they felt that anything they might say as someone who came from afar would just be further cultural appropriation.

Some at the complex had no rules they could recognize. They knew several who were like them from afar but who wrote novels that were set on the island that had characters from the island and who when they read their novels presented themselves as from the island without explaining that they were originally from afar or who presented themselves as representing the people of the island, as voicing the concerns of those who had genealogical ties to the island from before the whaling ships arrived. So one person they knew who was originally from the continent but had grown up on military bases on various islands was presented as the first novelist of these various islands by their publisher. They could not imagine that they thought of themself this way. Yet they were cavalier about their identity. They did not claim much but neither did they disclaim and so their identity slid around a lot and they got prizes for being an island novelist in contests on the continent and they showed up and accepted them.

Another writer also from afar was presented by their publisher as writing the first great novel of the island in the middle of the Pacific, the first novel to really capture the island and its peoples. They wrote novels in which their characters had names that suggested they were characters who had genealogical ties to the island from before the whaling ships arrived but when questioned about these characters they would claim that they were really from the continent and, they would assert, they had a freedom of expression, a freedom that let them tell the stories of anyone. This was true. They could tell the stories of any of them. None of them could really stop them. Yet it also seemed weird to them that this novelist from afar when confronted with complaints would not at least begin to think about why a colonized culture might feel protective of its stories, might want to protect them, keep them fresh, because they might be needed for resistance in the future.

There was much talk about the novel on the island, especially what would be or could be or might be the first novel of the island.

Or the first novel to really capture the island.

Or the first novel to really capture the island written by someone who had genealogical ties to the island from before the whaling ships arrived.

Or the first novel to really capture the island written by someone who had genealogical ties to the island from before the whaling ships arrived and who also stayed on the island to write.

Or the first novel to really capture the island written by someone who had genealogical ties to the island from before the whaling ships arrived and who also stayed on the island to write and who published their novel with an island press.

Or the first novel to really capture the island written by someone who had genealogical ties to the island from before the whaling ships arrived and who also stayed on the island to write and who published their novel with an island press and who wrote a novel that was a rousing call to arms for the end of the colonial occupation of the island.

This talk fascinated them because the novel had arrived like them from afar. It had arrived on the whaling ships. And for years when classes taught the novel of the island they taught it as written entirely by people from afar. There were some now who had genealogical ties to the island from before the whaling ships arrived who wrote the novel, but because the novel had such a machine of production around it these novels tended to be marketed to the continent and many who lived on the island did not see these novels as part of their tradition. And there was even some discussion about whether the island even needed a novel by someone with genealogical ties to the island from before whaling ships arrived or not. The culture had done so well without the novel, why would it want it?

Because they were poets, they thought a lot about how they were glad they did not write novels. But they knew also that just because they wrote poetry, a genre that had a long history on the island before the whaling ships arrived, they did not get off having to think about what it meant to be a poet on the island. Poetry it seemed was always in trouble with someone. Often the controversy made its way to the front page of the local newspapers even if the local newspapers did not really publish much poetry in them. Before they arrived there had been a controversy over a poem written by a poet who had genealogical ties to the island from before the whaling ships arrived and who was also an activist and whose activism and outspokenness caused extreme emotion in many. Often when they told those that they met in casual situations on the island that they worked at the complex, these people that they met would mention the poet activist's name to them with anger. They themselves did not feel this anger and these outbursts always made them feel uncomfortable. They felt that the poet activist had the right to say what they wanted to say and they admired their abilities to say things that other people would not say but might be thinking. This poet activist wrote a poem about a racist white woman that talked about kicking the face and puncturing the eyes of the racist white woman. When this book was published a student who was from afar, from the middle of the continent, made fun of this poem in the school newspaper in a cartoon. The cartoon showed the poet activist holding the book overhead as if it were an axe and madly screaming the poem at a cowering woman. Much controversy erupted from the poem and from the cartoon and this was just one of many ways that poetry mattered on the island. There was much debate about whether the poem was racist or not and then once this was not decided, if it was even possible for someone with genealogical ties to the island from before the whaling ships arrived to be racist to someone from afar or if a different term would be necessary to describe this sort of behavior. They often talked over beers about this poet and their poem with their friends from afar, their friends who were born on the islands but who had parents or grandparents from afar, and their friends who had genealogical ties to the island from before the whaling ships arrived. One friend who had genealogical ties to the island from before the whaling ships arrived said that the poem was not racist because it was about a specific woman and they named the woman's name and this woman was a well-known member of the administration of the complex who was notorious for saying racist things. Their friend felt that if the poem was not about all white women, it was not racist. Another friend who had like them come from afar said that it was about racism and thus wasn't racist. They were unsure about both of these positions. It seemed to them that the point of the poem was to slide one specific white woman over most white women and what they liked about the poem was how it swooped down and caught them in their white womanness. This did not make the poem racist but it did induce in them a profound dislocation. The poem made them nervous. It was how the history of the place caught them. Suddenly they and their values had positions that they did not realize they had before. It was just one more moment among many that brought them to an awareness that they had a race and were joined with others of this race. They had, obviously, always had a race. Anyone born after imperialism had a race foisted on them. Some of them managed to duck and dodge this imperial imposition but only by tricking it, by claiming to be a different race than the one that the imperial imposition wanted them to claim but no one could ever completely duck and claim that they had no race. But in the complex on the continent, while race was often discussed, their race was assumed to be the default position. So when they took courses in the literature of the continent, the literature was mainly written by haoles. And any view of the literature of the continent that presented it as not written mainly by haoles was usually taught in a separate course that had a hyphenated identity in the title of it. And when they talked among their friends about other haole friends they did not call them haoles, they just talked about them. But when they talked about their friends who were not haoles, they often identified them by one of the identity positions that had been imposed on them by imperialism. So moments like this, moments where they had to realize their white womanness, felt like a sudden relief. It was not that they wanted to stand up proud and declaim. It was more subtle and stupid. It was as if they had been walking around with their shirt on inside out and everyone had been looking at their shirt and wondering why it was on inside out but no one said anything and so they could not understand why they had been looking at their shirt until finally someone pointed out that their shirt was on inside out and then at that moment they suddenly understood what was going on.

It was not just poems of anger that caught their attention. Nature poetry also had a different resonance on the island. Many people around them were so moved by the island that they wrote poems celebrating nature. Sometimes people from afar arrived by plane, wrote a poem, and then left by plane. These poems were called 747 poems by those who did not leave by plane, those of all sorts who called the island home.

When they talked about poetry and the island with their friends, they could often be heard declaiming to anyone who would listen that nature poetry was the most immoral of poetries because it showed the bird, often a bird that like themselves had arrived from afar, and not the bulldozer. But when they looked more deeply at nature poetry, when they looked beyond the poems collected in anthologies that had images of the surf on the beach and looked instead at poems written by those who had deep connections to the islands, they realized a whole new use for nature poetry. They read a poem, for instance, that began as a nature poem with the koaʻe bird gliding over a volcano but the koaʻe turned into a plane as it glided over an urban part of the island filled with skyscrapers and ended with asphalt. This was a poem that included both precontact and postcontact nature in it and that split perspective changed the things they could say about nature poetry dramatically. And there was a song that was sung by a large falsetto singer that saw the land not only as something of great beauty but as something of great beauty that was at risk. The lyric had celebration and environmental and political critique in its simple words. It had it all and this all that it had gave them chills when they heard the song sung. And there was a creation chant of this island in the Pacific that was written before the whaling ships arrived that told the story of creation beginning from single cells. The chant began in slime then moved to coral polyp then grub then earthworm. What they found most moving about the chant was how it pointed out the connectedness of life for as the chant lists the creation of a number of animals and plants it lists one from the sea and one from the land so as to speak to the interconnected nature of land and sea. Reading this chant gave them light feelings of hope in their chest because they felt that to see the connection between land and sea is also to see how one nation's oil use could cause the disappearance of another's island. And they recognized nature poetry in these contexts not as immoral but as politicized, as telling the layers of history, and as a warning as the large falsetto singer sang in a lamenting, high voice, that our land is in great danger now.

After spending days that turned into months and then months that turned into years out in the sun of complication, a sun that exposed the very language they had learned from birth as not natural but as expansionist and a sun that taught them to entirely rethink poetry, a form of writing that they had written and read for years, they developed not only the reddening of a sunburn but also the dry mouth and throbbing head of heatstroke. So they began to make up a series of rules hoping they would work as a sort of shade that might deflect the light and would as a result allow them to stay out in the sun thinking. Their rules went like this . . . Whenever they discussed the island, they had the responsibility to address the legacy of colonialism on the island. They could never pretend that it did not shape their every sentence, their use of every word, their every comma, and their every period. They could not pretend that they were innocent of it, that they did not benefit from it all the time. They felt that any work that they did about the island should somehow make clear that it was against colonialism. But at the same time this work should also make clear that they were not the only person who had ever thought up anticolonialism. They had to point out both that they supported the sovereignty movement and that this movement was larger than them so as to indicate that while they supported the movement they were not its spokesperson and were not a major or crucial part of this movement. And they felt that they should never suggest in their work that they knew what form of government the people who had genealogical ties to the island from before the whaling ships arrived should use but they also felt that they should suggest as often as possible that the island should be governed by those who had genealogical ties to the island from before the whaling ships arrived and not by those from afar. They also felt they should not claim to understand the culture that was there before the whaling ships arrived. And if they were for some reason going to write something set in the past, they should not set any of their work in the time before the whaling ships arrived. And they felt they should make clear in their work that they were in dialogue with other writers from the island, they were not the only writer from the island or even the writer to read when one wanted to read about the island and that this dialogue might not even be dialogue because it might just be that they were influenced, not that they actually influenced anyone back. They felt they had to make clear when talking to people that their perspective on the island was just one among many and an incomplete one that they arrived at only by learning from others who had genealogical ties to the island from before the whaling ships arrived and others who were born on the island but had families and heritages from afar. So they wrote no poems about how beautiful the bougainvillea was without also mentioning how the plant was probably brought to the island in 1827 by the first Catholic missionary to the island. And during this time whenever they had to submit a biographical note to go with some publication they always wrote that they were a continential haole so as to make clear that they did not have genealogical ties to the island from before the whaling ships arrived but most of the editors of the publications on the continent edited out this information.

They did not think that their rules should be everyone else's rules or that other people had to sign on to them. They did not nail them to any door. And they tried hard not to complain about other people's differing rules with their friends. They respected the decision of their friend from afar not to teach creative writing even though they felt that creative writing at the complex could not change unless people who felt that it should be taught by those with genealogical ties to the island from before the whaling ship arrived taught it and then worked to hire those people because creative writing at the complex would not do this hiring without internal pressure. It for sure was not going to change on its own. And they also let their rules evolve and change over time. At some moments they let themselves mention the bougainvillea as if it were innocent or perhaps they skirted into dangerous territory by using the names of the animals and plants mentioned in a creation chant that was composed before the whaling ships arrived in their own work. At other moments they found themselves suddenly inserting the words of plants or animals in the language that was spoken on the island before the arrival of the expansionist language. Words like maiʻa, ʻulu, kukui, and kī, the words for plants like the banana, breadfruit, candlenut, and cordyline in the language that was spoken on the island before the whaling ships arrived that were brought over on canoes by the original settlers of the island, would suddenly appear in a poem about what people might carry with them. Or they found themselves describing themselves and people like them through metaphors of invasive alien plants. Like koa haole and huehue haole. And also trees like the kiawe that was brought to the island in the 1800s and grew so out of control that it was responsible for lowering the water tables all over the island. They justified this by saying that the ecological attentions of the culture that was on the island before the whaling ships arrived was so crucial it transcended culture, no one could own that field of knowledge. But they also recognized how they had broken one of their rules.

Sometimes others saw the rules and their continued desire to discuss the rules as guilt. Several of the editors of publications that edited out their declaration that they were a continental haole said that they did so because it read as guilt. So they thought a lot about guilt during this time. They began by wondering if there really was something wrong with guilt. After all, they were guilty of so many things. It was an endless list but right at the top of their list was the large amount of protein they and those near them ate, the large amount of oil they and those near them used, the large amount of pollutants they and those near them put in the air and in the ocean and on the land, the large number of people who had been killed in the name of freedom for them and those near them. They wondered if guilt was bad because it was an emotion of inaction, if it was really just all talk and no action as was often said. But they also thought that part of the reason things were so wrong was that not enough people felt guilty. And then they also noticed that the charge of guilt was used more often to stop people from action and conversely that guilt often moved people to action. And then they moved from thinking about guilt to thinking about complicity. Because what they really wanted was to constantly be saying they were complicit with all sorts of things, even things that happened without their consent but happened nonetheless and continued to happen also without their consent.

As much as they felt uncomfortable on the island, when they went back to the continent, they still felt uncomfortable. Most of this discomfort was political. Not infrequently someone on the continent would say to them that they should not live on the island where they lived because haoles had done enough damage. While they admired the politics of these people, they always felt weird that these people could not see the history of where they were standing and how it was a similar history of loss of land and continued disenfranchisement. But they also felt uncomfortable among their friends who did not think about colonialism all the time when they would return to the continent. So uncomfortable it was hard to hang out with them. They found their friendships with their friends on the continent to suddenly be haunted by the political infection and they only wanted to hang out with those who also had the same infection. It was just more comfortable this way. People who they had previously found politically overreactive and shrill suddenly felt comfortable. People who felt comfortable previously they suddenly felt to be part of the problem. They felt annoyed when their friends did not want to discuss colonialism or did not want to go to the African film festival because they did not like that sort of stuff. What sort of stuff they would say defensively. It was like nationalism. They had been against it as they were for the radical at one time. But now they saw it as a tool, one that could liberate and repress, like most tools. And they felt obligated not to dismiss it too easily. They cringed when a poet critic sent them a paper in which they kept talking about all of American poetry as if it was one whole thing and they said that American poetry is guilty of nationalism when they meant something more like jingoism. Or when their work appeared in an anthology and in the anthology it was said that what was good about the work in the anthology was that it was anti-nationalist. They knew these feelings were silly, unfair, even damaging to their relationships with kind people. But they continued to find it impossible to talk about aesthetics without also talking about who took over whom. It was like nature poetry. It enraged them if it didn't somehow address the constant human destruction of various habitats.

But at times, despite their attention to the rules, despite all their attempts to find firm footing for themselves around this issue of appropriation, they found themselves at moments feeling as if they could never find their way. One afternoon they went to an all-day conference on globalization and at the conference a scholar who had genealogical ties to the island from before the whaling ships arrived spoke and said the state should disallow writing on the people or the culture of the people who had genealogical ties to the islands from before whaling ships arrived unless the writer had ties to the islands from before the whaling ships arrived. They called on the complex and the state government to set up rules that said that any such work should be approved by a board made up of people who had genealogical ties to the island from before the whaling ships arrived. They wondered, once again, as they listened to their talk if their talk was more performance than anything else. They were after all requesting that the state and its complex commit huge infringements on the First Amendment rights of state workers and even if they were fine with that, their request was impossible to enforce. But still their saying this made them feel nervous about their own work despite all the time they had spent obsessively thinking about and revising their rules. They could just dismiss the scholar. Just say they were yet another example of ethnic nationalism and look what ethnic nationalism had done to the twentieth century. But they felt that this dismissal would also be missing a point, or a series of complicated points about the long history of constant yet profoundly unequal exchanges that had defined the thinking on and about the island. They felt at this moment that they could never have enough rules. They felt caught between the one or the other. They felt caught between their feeling that the responsible thing to do was to be attentive to the issues that so defined the island and yet at the same time they also worried that they had no right to talk about the island.

Again and again they felt as if they could not escape, that whatever they did was wrong. They could never sort through the layers of history. They could never feel things in the same way that those who were born on the island might feel them, whether those people had genealogical ties to the island from before the whaling ships arrived or not. They did not know what it meant to breathe the island air with its slightly higher quality than the continent for years. They did not know what it meant to eat food grown in the specific island soils and its varying degrees of wetness and dryness. They did not know what it meant to feel the intensity of the sun in this place warming their skin year after year. They knew these things only for a short amount of time, which meant they barely knew them. And this feeling of never enough rules, never enough lived knowledge, overwhelmed them into a sort of depressed inaction and they realized that despite their obsessive thinking about and revising of rules they had trouble answering hard yet obvious questions about their work. When a friend who had genealogical ties to the island from before the whaling ships arrived asked them who they wrote for, they realized that they barely thought about this question and it was hard to figure out the answer. They finally admitted that they guessed they wrote for themselves. They wrote for themselves because they wrote to figure out things that they could not figure out otherwise, things they could not figure out just by thinking. They needed writing. They needed poetry because it reshaped their mind, because it resorted things in different, sometimes beautiful, sometimes troubling patterns. They especially needed poetry to think with others, to think with the traditions of the island, to think beside them and near them but not as part of them. They needed poetry to be able to think about the relationship between the scrubby and ugly koa haole with its brown bean pods that was crowding out the beautiful endemic 'ohai with its small red heart-shaped flowers. They wished they could say that they wrote for themselves and for strangers. But it seemed presumptuous to say they wrote for strangers, at least for strangers on the island. They agreed with a friend from the continent who had genealogical ties to the continent from before the exploratory ships arrived on the continent that if they wrote about another culture, a culture at risk because of colonialism and a culture that was not theirs really, the writing should give something back to the culture. But it also felt presumptuous to think they could give anything back. The culture was so rich and so complete without them.

At this same conference on globalization a scholar who like them was from afar but who had lived on the island for many years gave a talk. Their talk was about the ocean. They had an understanding of the ocean as also at risk, but at risk because of human interference and human refusal to see the connections between all the parts of the ocean. They saw clearly how humans refused to understand that when they dumped waste into one part of the ocean they dumped it into all of the ocean; how when they fished out one part of the ocean, they fished out the entire ocean. They ended their talk by begging them to remember the ocean, to just remember the ocean amidst all their fighting. At this time they found this so moving, this gentle reminder to remember the ocean in the frail and small voice of an elderly man. Remembering the ocean, by which they meant remembering the devastation of the ocean that had happened in the last twenty years, they thought again about place, about the responsibilities of writing to place. And thus they continued to circle around and around in their thinking and the sun shone down and their skin sometimes tanned and their skin sometimes burned.

6

Then one of them moved. And that changed things.

One of them moved from the island in the Pacific to an island in the Atlantic. Two of them stayed on the island in the Pacific.

One of them moved because they felt the prickly new cells making their body rigid, making their face red. It was not that they denied the infection. It was the opposite. They embraced the infection and they agreed they were a huge part of the problem and because they were a part of the problem they agreed to buy a one-way ticket off the island. They were unlike the other two of them who stayed. The two of them who stayed were flushed and feverish from the infection and thus somewhat addicted to oscillating between confusion, excitement, and despair. If offered a drug to lower their fever they would have refused it; the fever intensified their vision and their dreams and thus it felt as if it gave their life a meaning.

But because one of them refused to live with the infection, refused to live on the island in the Pacific with all its thought and its histories, they agreed to begin physically careening back and forth for a few years between various islands and climates and cultures. They still liked each other and still wanted to be near each other, so they spent the fall and spring on the island in the Pacific and then the summer and some of the winter on the island in the Atlantic. The island in the Atlantic to which one of them moved was one thousand, three hundred and thirty-seven square miles. It was nestled beside a continent and it was connected by bridges and tunnels to the continent as well as to two other islands. The islands were points of entry and had all the economic advantages that points of entry have. And these islands were so close together that people moved among the islands all day long effortlessly.

Their moving back and forth between the island in the Atlantic and the island in the middle of the Pacific was seen by some as a privileged existence. A friend who lived on the continent but was from afar, from a small island nation in the Pacific with a long history of occupation by other nations, joked that they were like certain painters and writers from the turn of the century who went by ship to various islands in the Pacific and painted or wrote about these locations with a wistful exoticism. But instead of feeling wistful they constantly felt as if they were in the wrong place, felt like they said or thought the wrong thing no matter where they were. They would say something that they thought would be okay on one island in one ocean only to remember that they were on the other island in the other ocean and this thing was the wrong thing to say on the other island. Or that was how it felt. The list of things was probably more in their mind than anything else but that didn't make it any less endless or real to them. They felt that Woody Allen films were okay in the Atlantic but not in the Pacific. Nationalism was okay in the Pacific but not in the Atlantic. The avant-garde was okay in the Atlantic but not in the Pacific. Rigid identity politics as strategic essentialism okay in the Pacific but not in the Atlantic. Immigration okay in the Atlantic but vexed in the Pacific. Mormonism okay in the Pacific but not in the Atlantic. The list went on and on, irony and urban density and emotion about the land and localism and globalism and jokes about Samoans and jokes about Poles . . .

It wasn't that they valued being chameleonlike and never wanted to think anything disagreeable or risky, but it was as if they couldn't get the elaborate cultural rituals of jokes quite right in their confusion about who they were and where they belonged or just where they were at a certain moment. They knew that they should tell jokes. Jokes were told around them all day long on both the islands. But they were like a parent's friend whom they remembered from childhood, a kindly but pathetic parent's friend who attempted to ingratiate themselves with whomever was in their general vicinity by endlessly telling jokes but it was as if they did not understand the basic rules of joke telling and so they of English heritage was constantly blundering, telling they of Irish heritage a joke about the Irish man and light bulbs. Or they would attempt to ingratiate themselves with a group of women by telling them a joke about how two breasts go into a bar and what one breast says to the other breast.

The moving back and forth not only confused them but it wore them down. It was both physically and emotionally hard. So to get rid of this feeling, the feeling of disorientation, the two of them that were living on the island in the Pacific decided to move to the island in the Atlantic. They also moved to be near the one who refused to live on the island in the Pacific. They moved for love, for desire, for friendship. And they moved for other reasons also, reasons they couldn't fully articulate to themselves but instead felt in the gray matter at the backs of their brains. This gray matter held things up front like desires to have less sides to themselves and desires to have less emotion about the place where they lived and also desires to be surrounded by people who like them moved around a lot and somewhat valued the moving around as a way of learning about things even as they saw the limitations of this moving around such as a certain rootlessness or a certain lack of historical perspective or a certain inability to understand the ecosystems of a place. The gray matter would say to them that part of the move was just a desire to spend less time on planes, less time in cramped seats with twitchy legs breathing stale air and trying to sleep. But really these thoughts were only what the gray matter allowed the front of their brain to comprehend.

The gray matter at the back of their brain told them to move to the islands in the Atlantic because the islands were known for their perversions and various sexualities and they wanted to live someplace known for its perversions and various sexualities. The gray matter at the back of the brain wanted to move to the place that self-identified as a place of complicated sexuality, a place for people who liked to be getting in and out of various beds in various different ways. A place that celebrated different beds and different ways of bedding down and around. The islands in the Atlantic, were full of perversions of all sorts and the stories told about the people of the islands had all the genders in all the different combinations, even the ones beyond the two that so defined their culture at this moment. They liked this. They liked it that the islands in the Atlantic to which they moved were so famous for their perversions, so famous that televangelists mentioned them often as the root of all evil. In the hometown of one of them, many called the islands in the Atlantic Sodom and the rest in this town called them Gomorrah. And this is what so attracted the gray matter at the back of their brain to the city. This was it.

The front of their brain did not admit that this is what attracted them. And if asked, the front of their brain would have disowned it. It would have pointed out that their sex life was not as glittering as the sex life of the characters in the various television shows that were shown about the islands in the Atlantic that featured wealthy, vain, and self-centered characters of unusually distinctive beauty. Their sex life had no shiny sheets or group showers or accidental pregnancies after one-night stands. It was slower and more private than all this. It had lots of laundry and house cleaning in it. The front of their brain liked to think that their sex life had more respect in it and less panting. But sometimes it had more panting and less respect.

But when it came down to it, neither the front nor the back of their brain knew what to say about their relations with one another. They tried not to talk about it as a result. And then when they did talk about it, both parts of the brain worked together to do so in the most boring way possible. They used detached pronouns or they wrote poems where they described in great detail impossible sexual positions as a metaphor for the impossibility they felt in their own life or they were just really vague and hoped no one would notice.

But still that their sexual lives were shaped around triangles rather than straight lines did shape their lives, made the back of their brain realize that it wanted to live in certain places and not in others. Made it known that they wanted to live in a city of perversion and variety so they could disappear into all the variety and not worry about what others thought.

Basically the gray parts of their brain denied the prickly new cells and ignored the fever as best it could. And it told them a story in which they were heroes for leaving. They were heroes for buying a one-way ticket off the island. They were heroes for moving to a place where they could call themselves perverts and have it be a badge of honor, not a colonial concept. Basically, their brain was lying to them. And they knew it. Their brain ignored that the islands in the Atlantic also had a history where people came from afar and set up their own form of government, an inefficient and unfair one. Their brain pretended as if they were no longer colonizers on the islands in the Atlantic but instead were immigrants. They no longer characterized people as having genealogical ties or as being from afar because they knew only three people who both had genealogical ties to the island in the Atlantic from before the exploratory ships arrived and presented those ties as an integral part of who they were.

No matter, they let their brain lie to them; they embraced delusion and moved. They packed up lies with their stuff into cardboard boxes and they carried them down to the post office to be shipped to the island in the Atlantic on a boat. Then they got on a plane with more lies in their carry-ons, and this plane flew off the island in one of the flight patterns that they could have seen from their lanai, had they been there on their lanai at that moment instead of sitting in the plane in a small compact seat.

Ten hours then passed in a haze of sleeping pills and salty food and then the plane landed on an island in the Atlantic.

The minute they got off the plane they began trying to figure out what it meant to be there on an island in the Atlantic. They began by comparing the two islands. Both islands they noticed were full of concrete and very tall buildings. Both were dense with people. Both had oversized roles in the cultural imaginations of many. The island in the Pacific was known for beauty and for the military. The other in the Atlantic was known for world culture, for immigration, and for finance. Both had colonial histories. Both were occupied by the same government. Both had been taken over by men who had arrived from afar on ships. Both had high land prices. Both places had a changed ecosystem as the result of birds originally from afar that were released by those who came from afar.

At the airport, they got into a car and as they rode in the car from the airport to the apartment they thought of the list of things they were moving to. They were moving to a connection with other islands and the continent; they were moving to being able to go between things; they were moving to a certain roughness and destruction for the islands in the Atlantic were known for their toughness, for their guns, for their drugs, for their projects, for the dirtiness of their subways, for their organized crime, for their loudness and extremes, for putting great wealth and great poverty on the same street corner. And at the same time they were moving to the certain, very specific beauty of the islands in the Atlantic. They were moving to the sun hitting the side of an old building and the very brick in the building lighting up with a certain sheen that was luminous and impossible to describe but deeply glowed as if the wealth of the industry in the buildings was so great that it seeped into the very mortar. They were moving to a horizon and then a spread of lights at night over this horizon, a horizon with so many levels and so much depth and so much wideness.

One of them had a father who had been a singer on one of the islands for a while. They had sung songs in burlesque clubs and as one of them grew up they sang to them, half in parody and half in celebration, songs about the city. They would sing words such as if you can make it there, you can make it anywhere to them in their beds late at night when they were a child in the middle of the continent. And while they knew that they hadn't really made it there, as at the time they lived in a small rural town in the middle of the continent, a town without libraries or bookstores, they still listened to the words of those songs with a sleepily mesmerized intentness as if they were in a language they could understand if only they concentrated because they couldn't imagine at the time such a place of privilege, a place so privileged that it told people that they had made it or not anywhere. At the time that their father sang these songs, they were living in a town where the highest building would eventually be six stories tall and at the time of the singing that building hadn't even been built yet. Later in their life, they thought a lot about this six-story-tall building even as they felt they were at a risk of overthinking it. But they couldn't stop from seeing it as a metaphor. The buildings in their town didn't have bricks that glowed. It wasn't that the buildings had no aesthetic. But it was that they had a different aesthetic, one more transitory and utilitarian. There, buildings were not built out of hope but out of need. Which was fine. This place where they had grown up had an entirely different set of issues to deal with but it did explain why they were so caught up in tall buildings and their bricks and their steel girders, a caught-up-ness that was not without its critiques or hesitations, not without its suspicions. But the caught-up-ness was one part of the beginning of an explanation of why they moved from the islands in the Pacific to the islands in the Atlantic.

Once they arrived at the apartment, they carried in their bags and they began the process of getting settled. They got settled by thinking more and more about how the islands in the Atlantic were all about wideness and had a specific beauty of stability and time and solidity, a beauty that was different but as moving as the beauty of the lighter green leaf canopy of the kukui.

While on the island in middle of the Pacific, they zoomed in and noticed the luminous beauty of leaf texture and the interconnections and power relationships among plants growing on top of one another, but while on the islands in the Atlantic they spent all their time looking up and down avenues and streets, focusing on the distance, noticing the lines of bridges and the dialogue that the uneven heights of buildings in a row had with the air above them. They noticed filled space and empty space.

There was so much height and then within that height so many humans and so much motion that they couldn't zoom in at all and so they had to let all the height and the people and the motion flood into their minds; they had to open their minds to wideness. They had to open their minds to a different, dirtier, layered beauty. They had to open their minds to a beauty of different and contradictory ideas. To a beauty of lostness and never feeling fluent but feeling that that was fine, that that was part of being in this place and that one was in this place of lostness, without fluency with a whole bunch of other people. This ability to recognize one's self as lost and belonging with the others in the lostness, this is what made the place matter, what brushed off on them and made them matter and everyone around them matter also. Just standing in line at the post office, they heard many different languages, languages full of meaning and histories that they couldn't even recognize, guttural languages, languages that clicked, other languages that had rhythms too intricate for their middle-of-the-continent ears to hold in their minds as anything but an unusual, unrecognizable, and thus beautiful song. These islands in the Atlantic were so layered and so full of so many from so many different places that various weird fevers were brought to the islands from other places by the constant movement. If there was a plague or a virus or a bug or an animal-borne illness in any one corner of the globe, then someone at any one moment on the islands probably had it. Yet because the islands' residents were known for their resilience, they just took this up as yet another story they told themselves about the greatness of the islands. And it was true, although whether it was great or not they could not say, that the traffic through the islands felt as if it carried a huge part of all the information that it was possible for humans to carry. And as the islands were so small in size and so dense with people who were constantly brushing up against one another and touching and pushing each other into and out of the subway and up the stairs and then out into more people, there was a constant exchange of air in and out of each others lungs. So they got to the island in the Atlantic and they too began to breathe with others.

They let the beauty of the one and the other seep into them while ignoring how the island in the Atlantic had the one or the other as much as other places. This was a place that told grandiose stories about itself, told others that it was a place to which people moved and it didn't matter how long you were at this place, that this place was for people from all over. Yet this wasn't really true. This place, like the island in the middle of the Pacific, was a place colonized by people who came from afar in ships and who set up their own form of government, an inefficient and unfair one. Over two hundred years later, this government continued to occupy all these various islands and the continent near them and it had set up very restrictive rules and complicated passport-checking booths at the borders to prevent large numbers of people from moving into the islands and the continent, to prevent large numbers of people from other places from using up the wealth that the government that currently occupied the island and the continent had accumulated at the expense of others on the planet. And even those who got past the complicated passport-checking booths were still caught in the unforgiving economy and unfair hiring practices of this economy that was controlled by the government that currently occupied the continent. They still had to deal with the police force of the government that currently occupied the continent and the tendency of this police force to physically abuse and shoot those who were both from afar and having trouble with the unforgiving economy of the government that currently occupied the continent. So while it was somewhat true that there was a difference between the islands in the Atlantic and the islands in the Pacific and that difference was that being born on one of the islands in the Atlantic had no extra meaning, granted no apparent special privileges, was rarely even discussed, it was still a place that granted privileges to some and not to others. While it was a city that celebrated the swarming movements of people, it only celebrated the swarming movements of certain people.

They lived on one of the larger islands near the smaller, more dense, and most prosperous island. They moved to one of the larger islands because the rent was cheaper on this island and so most of their friends lived on the island. They settled into an apartment with an upstairs and a downstairs. One of them had a desk downstairs. Two of them shared a room with two desks upstairs. They all set up their computers and one of them built a network that connected all the computers. Each of them had folders on their computers that contained shared files and also folders that were password protected. In the shared files they kept photographs and music and fonts and in the password protected files they kept poetry and diaries and letters.

There were other things in this apartment. There were two rooms with beds. One bed was softer and one bed was harder. One bedroom, the bedroom of the harder bed, was full of light and had a tree outside the window and various sorts of city birds lived in the tree and sang city birdsongs in the morning. One bedroom, the bedroom of the softer bed, was a room in another room and no light from the outside entered it and it often got stuffy in the night when the doors were closed.

They got used to each other again at these desks and in these bedrooms. And they entered into the world of mundane worries and fights about who should take out the garbage and who had to sort the recycling and who had to clean the bathroom and beneath all this mundaneness they had dreams in their soft and hard beds. One of them dreamed of being crushed by two big blue rubber balls and that in order to stop the crushing they had jump up and breathe and then hold their breath and jump down under water, beneath the balls, and swim out. But in the dream they were afraid to swim out under the water even though it would have been easy. Instead they just stood there letting the two big blue rubber balls hit them in the face. One of them dreamed that they were getting a tattoo of birds such as the hedge sparrow, the dipper, the peacock, the ostrich, and the bird of paradise, all of them in flight or walking, whatever the individual bird's preference, in a circle around their upper arm. One of them dreamed about Three Dog Night and the Three Stooges and opening and closing doors.

Their dreams were pressing but this period of moving from one place to another place and having this motion take over their thoughts the way metaphor takes over poems was only a brief period. A period of some two months or so. During these months there were other things that they thought about and they thought about them because of the infection with its prickly new cells that they had caught on the island in the middle of the Pacific. They thought about steel and concrete as invented, mongrel products. They thought about how the islands added concrete to themselves at the rate of one Hoover Dam every eighteen months. They thought about the starlings released into Central Park by Eugene Schiffelin, a man who founded an acclimatization society in order to introduce to the continent that has the Atlantic on one side and the Pacific on the other all the birds in Shakespeare's plays. They thought about the monk parrots that may or may not have escaped from a crate at an airport and now lived on the larger of the islands in the Atlantic where they built three-story homes of twigs along the power lines. They thought about the warm-weather plants that aclimatically thrived in the area because of the heat that collected in the city's large amount of concrete. They thought about the triggerfish, parrotfish, queen angels, butterfly fish, sergeant majors, spotfins, angelfish, damselfish, groupers, squirrelfish, trumpetfish, and all the other tropical fish that were washed up onto the waters off the islands by the Gulf Stream each spring.

One of them was at this time developing a sort of environmental anxiety, an anxiety that may have been anxiety or may have been completely rational as they had lived for so many years on the island in the Pacific, an island with one of the highest concentrations of species death in the world, and so they liked to think during this period about how things continue to grow and mutate against all odds and they found these thoughts a pacifying balm. They liked to think about how some small plants still grow in the cracks between the concrete. They liked to think of the stability of the city's buildings and yet how the stability was illusory. Someone had told them that if the humans went away, it would only take one hundred years for the land to become someplace where concrete was not dominant. They liked to think on this. They were not sure how much longer the humans would be around making concrete and they didn't like to think that concrete had to be there forever after humans were gone. They would rather it were not there at all. But it was there and so as a result they liked to think about how things might continue on without humans, as it seemed to be only a matter of time before humans had made the planet uninhabitable for humans. As a meditation practice to cope with this anxiety they would sit in a chair looking out the window at the street. They would sit in a chair and breathe in the concrete and then breathe out an image of grasses and trees growing out of the concrete, breathe in the street and breathe out an image of roots breaking the concrete apart, breathe in the cars and breathe out collapsing and neglected freeway overpasses and with this meditation practice they were convinced all would be well.

7

Then they woke up one morning and the sky was clear and the air warm and an airplane had been driven into the side of one of the tallest buildings in the world, a building that was located on the denser island in the Atlantic. They realized this because they had turned on the television to see the weather for the day and instead saw a burning building. Then a few minutes later another airplane was driven into the building beside the first building. They watched this on television but they also heard it, heard a loud sound off in the distance.

Then they went outside and stood on the corner. The corner had a straight view down the street to the buildings. Others from the neighborhood had already gathered there. The neighborhood was full of both projects and brownstones and so the demographics of the neighborhood were variable and as a result there was a crowd of older people and younger people from a range of classes and races standing on the corner. All these people wore different sorts of clothing that declared their allegiances to their various classes and races as they stood together on the far corner looking at the burning buildings. They were mainly silent. One of them had a tape recorder and said they were from an independent media source. They circulated among them asking their reactions. They avoided them because they did not know what to say. How could they know what to say? They couldn't even process what had happened. They just stood there looking. Then they turned away to go buy an egg sandwich from the store on the corner. They turned away and as they turned away they heard everyone gasp. They turned back and all they saw was a huge cloud of dust. They looked at the huge cloud of dust but they could not process what the dust might mean. They turned to the person next to them, the person with the microphone and the tape recorder, and asked them what had happened and they said that the building had fallen. Their words broke some spell, allowed them to all at once see the cloud of dust as concrete and steel, allowed them to hear the words of those around them that they couldn't hear before. Suddenly it seemed as if everyone started talking and moving. The people next to them said things like I'm getting out of here and this is too fucking weird. People began to scatter back to their homes. Another building remained burning and yet to fall but they left with the others and went back to their house and to the television where things were more mediated. The television was still on in their house when they got there but a few minutes later they heard a loud noise and then it filled with static or the television filled with static and then they heard a loud noise. Later when they retold their story of where they were when the buildings fell, which they would do over and over in the weeks to come, they couldn't say which happened first. But they realized then that the second building had fallen.

After the buildings fell down, one of them, the one who had not yet gone to work, kept wanting to go to work. And the other of them, the one who did not have a job, kept saying that this was impossible because martial law would soon be declared and it would be better to be on the larger island where they lived than on the more densely populated and smaller island where two of them worked. The one who wanted to go to work kept saying don't be so extreme; no martial law was declared in 1993 when the same building was bombed. Then the other replied, wake up; the tallest buildings in the city just fell down; things are different now.

What neither of them realized in their anxious bickering was how both of them were right in their wrongnesses. No martial law would be declared. But something more insidious was beginning right at that moment and it would take over. Sometimes it would blatantly show all of itself, show itself as a giant monster with many arms and several heads, the sort of giant monster that in the movies tended to come out of nowhere and engulf the two indulging in a panting embrace in an empty locker room. Yet at other moments in the months to come it would just creep in silently. It would be too big to be called by a single name like the Homeland Security Act or the Patriot Act or any of those operations that were to come, such as Operation Enduring Freedom, Operation Anaconda, Operation Snipe, Operation Mountain Lion, Operation Mountain Sweep, Operation Mountain Storm, Operation Valiant Strike, Operation Mountain Viper, and Operation Mountain Blizzard. At any one moment in the months and years to come, only certain parts of this large thing that was being made of this short moment would be clear and obvious. They would never see the whole picture. Even when they would look at this thing in months to come, they would only be able to see the tips of it. Certain parts of it would always be hidden and all the more powerful as a result. As they stood there in their room calling and locating their friends, sorting through their confusions and fears relentlessly but attaining no relief, there were government officials who stood elsewhere and who saw this confusion and fear in them standing in their room as a chance to start killing people in other places using in the name of this killing words such as freedom and patriotism. This would all become obvious when the government that currently occupied the continent would suddenly begin to hold people without a trial on an island in the middle of the Atlantic, when in the months after the buildings fell the government that currently occupied the continent interviewed five thousand men who had parents or grandparents who were from the area that extends from the eastern Mediterranean Sea to the Persian Gulf just because of the place of origin of their parents or grandparents, when a few years later smiling soldiers of the military that currently occupied the continent held up their thumbs as they dragged around naked prisoners with dog chains, as they posed next to a beaten body that was wrapped in ice.

But while they stood on the street corner, a time began, a time that lasted until Halloween. In this time little felt normal. At first the city had no airplanes coming or going for a few days, only military jets that flew over the city in regular patterns. And this feeling that they couldn't get out, couldn't get away from the military jets, made them upset. When they were on the island in the middle of the Pacific, airplanes had felt hopeful to them. They liked to sit on their lanai and watch the airplanes take off in a slow lumbering arc over the city. They liked to imagine the people leaving, sitting in those small, tight seats thinking about returning home to their comfortable beds after a vacation that had probably been somewhat disappointing because they had come to the island in the middle of the Pacific full of thoughts about deserted beaches and welcoming natives and then had gotten to the island and realized most of the beaches were full of concrete and surrounded by forty-story hotels with a staff that served them with a tight-lipped smile that showed no welcome, only a just-beneath-the-surface anger. Airplanes were a comfort then. They took them to a home.

But later, after the buildings fell down, airplanes became something different. When the flights started again, the flight patterns of the airplanes over the islands in the Atlantic changed. Suddenly the planes began to pass low over their yard. They would sit out in the cool backyard at night and watch them pass by. Their backyard on the island in the Atlantic lacked the view of the slow, lumbering arc in the perfectly framed window that had made the airplanes so full of hope on their lanai on the island in the middle of the Pacific. Here in the backyard in the Atlantic, the planes zoomed overhead, showing their bellies. The planes had a peculiar whine, a whine so loud that when they were in bed they would start awake as the airplanes passed overhead filled with hubristic worry that they were going to fly into them. Or they would see an airplane in the distance and become convinced that it was going into a building and their body would tense up with worry that they had to see this again. They tried to resist these thoughts. But once they resisted these thoughts other thoughts would occur. So if their brain told them that the planes were just following an unusual flight pattern, that the planes were highly unlikely to fly into any building, then another different thought would pop up and they would wonder if the airplanes were made to fly close down over their part of the city because it was so populated and this would drive more of them in this city to fear and make more of them support the awful operations and invasions to come with names like Operation Southern Focus, Operation Iraqi Freedom, Operation Planet X, Operation Peninsula Strike, Operation

Desert Scorpion, Operation Scorpion Sting, Operation Spartan Scorpion, Operation Rifles Scorpion, and Operation Sidewinder that were to come. They tried to see their fear as a militaristic plot so they could refuse it but instead what happened was that it boomeranged around and hit them in the back of their head over and over and as it did this it eventually shaped the gray matter of their brain into a knot of tightness. They could not get this knot to loosen, no matter how much breathing in of the concrete and then breathing out an image of grasses and trees growing out of the concrete they did. Even when they eventually began to sleep through the planes passing overhead, the planes showed up in their dreams. A plane would crash in their backyard and the backyard would be burning in their dream. Or in their dream they would be sitting on their lanai on the island in the middle of the Pacific filled with that calm feeling that watching the planes and their slow lumbering arc over the city against the clear blue sky induced in them and suddenly the planes would begin tumbling in strange and unusual patterns.

At the same time, despite the knot of tightness in the gray matter of their brain, they knew it would be absurd to claim that the buildings falling down was a big event. It was an awful event in the way that any bombing done by any government is an awful event, but it was not a big event. In terms of deaths resulting from containers filled with explosive materials, it barely registered on the world's top-ten list. There had been, after all, a lot of bombing over the years. People had been bombing each other since 1911 when Giulio Cavotti dropped a hand grenade out of the cockpit of his plane and onto Tagiura. No, earlier. Ever since the formula for gunpowder became known in 1044. Ever since the fragmentation bomb was invented in the fifteenth century. And the government that currently occupied the continent was very skilled at bombing. If they counted the numbers, if that mattered, the two thousand eight hundred and one dead was nothing next to the over one hundred and forty thousand who died in Hiroshima, the seventy thousand in Nagasaki.

Or another way to put it was that it was a small event with big consequences. The big consequences went beyond the obvious. Those who had loved someone who died and those who had been loved by someone who died obviously felt the event as enormous, enormous in the way that any death of someone who loves or who is loved by someone feels enormous. And so while there were two thousand eight hundred and one dead, and while each of those dead were loved by many others, many who were dealing with a huge hole in their heart that they did not in any way want to belittle, the city went on. It went on with a difference, but it did go on. And even though they wanted to not be changed by the buildings falling down, even though they liked to think of themselves as immune from public sentiment because they equated public sentiment with being caught in the desire to bomb someone in another continent, they could not deny that the event changed them and everyone around them in various ways. It changed them and everyone around them even as they said to themselves that it was stupid to say that everything had been changed, even as they said to themselves over and over that the event was not so big an event. And at the same time it was stupid to deny that the event changed them. They could see changes in themselves and those around them. To not acknowledge that the fallen buildings changed things meant not acknowledging the lumbering machine holding those from other places without a trial on a base on an island in the middle of the Atlantic, how the government that currently occupied the continent interviewed five thousand men who had parents or grandparents who were from the area that extends from the eastern Mediterranean Sea to the Persian Gulf just because of the place of origin of their parents or grandparents, the presence to come of the smiling soldiers of the military that currently occupied the continent holding up their thumbs as they dragged around naked prisoners with dog chains, as they posed next to a beaten body that was wrapped in ice, and the endless operations with names like Operation Soda Mountain, Operation Ivy Serpent, Operation Iron Bullet, Operation Tyr, Operation Ivy Lightning, Operation Silverado, Operation Ivy Needle, Operation Longstreet, and Operation Tiger Clean Sweep that were beginning and would continue. And it also meant not acknowledging how they acted in various ways that they had not acted before. Among their close friends, they had one friend who after the buildings fell down traveled by day with a group of friends who all slept together each night in a different apartment. And another who just got more and more shrill, more and more confident in their statements that it was the end of the world. And another who kept saying over and over that they were handling it better than everyone else when it was so obvious that they were not handling it better than everyone else and the evidence of this was how loudly and frequently they kept proclaiming that they were handling it better than everyone else. Other friends just worked through it all slowly and quietly in their own way.

And in their own house each of them were changed in different ways. One of them searched the internet hour after hour charting out the reasons for the airplanes flying into the buildings. They would find some fact, some detail about the government that currently occupied the continent, some connection, some numbers, some analysis and they would call them out all day long, call them out to the others who lived in the apartment. Call out the facts into the room. They would call out the suspected mastermind of the buildings falling down and their connections with the government that currently occupied the country. They would call out the sources of various arms in various enemy hands. They also began collecting the numbers of people whom the military that currently occupied the continent had killed in other countries. They made charts. Charts of killings as a result of bombings. Charts of probable indirect killings. Charts of killings done by coups supported by the military that currently occupied the continent. Charts of killings done by arms sold by companies based on the continent. Charts of killings done by technologies developed by companies based on the continent. Then a grand total that grew and grew and became unbearable to look at but was printed out in a large font on a single sheet of paper and posted on the wall by the desk.

Another of them just got lost. They just got lost. That was it. They had no chart to make. They didn't really want to leave the house and sleep with the roving group who moved from apartment to apartment and they knew they weren't handling it better than everyone else. They watched a lot of television once it came back on even though the television that returned was full of static and often required repeated antenna adjustments because the broadcast tower that they had used before the buildings had fallen had been on top of the one of the buildings. So now as they watched television they would get up repeatedly and adjust the antenna, move it a little to the right, and then they would sit back down, only to get up a few seconds later and move the antenna a little to the left. They did this for hours and in between the endless antenna adjustments they got lost while watching the well-lit pile of debris from the fallen buildings being moved around by bulldozers night after night on television. They just sat on the couch and watched. They watched humans climbing around in the big piles of debris. They looked at the skeleton frames of the buildings. They watched the president arrive and a whole crowd of people chant USA over and over, feeling slightly sick as they watched this. When they tired of watching television they turned to the internet and they looked at the cloud of smoke that continued to hover over the lower part of the island for many days. They found a site that reproduced satellite images and they took some comfort from looking at the smoke from space. While looking at the immense pile of rubble horrified them into a depressed trance, the wide-angle view from above took them out of themselves, took them out of the images of the very small men next to the very big pieces of building, took them away from the chants of USA, USA that happened when the president of the government that currently occupied the continent went to the pile of rubble and they again had that feeling of floating over the timeline of history. The picture that formed in their minds as they floated over all the history was of a timeline of killing. The timeline was long and there were many dots that marked times of killing. The timeline was just one dot after another and as they floated they recognized that they lived in a time that was just one more small dot on this timeline. Once they let their bodies float up over what was happening now, they could see what was happening now as one small turn in the plot of history. They knew that humans fought. They knew that humans fought over resources and they fought over beliefs. Although none of this fighting made any sense to them and they could not imagine killing any other of them because some they told them to kill them. But this thought that humans fight and have often fought and always fought let them float above the events, above the air, let them detach from it all, let them see it as part of being human, the scary part of being human, but part of being human nonetheless and as they too were human, wanted to be human, they had to deal with this part of being human. This comforted them but it also made them wonder if it was true, if they should stop reading the history and instead perhaps read more about the outbreak of tuberculosis that selectively killed off the biggest, nastiest, and most despotic males in the baboon troop and thus allowed a cultural swing toward pacifism, a relaxing of the usually parlous baboon hierarchy, and a willingness to use affection and mutual grooming rather than threats, swipes, and bites to foster a patriotic spirit. Or all those articles about the ant and its social stomach of sharing and those about how the lone wolf was a pack animal and not really a lone wolf at all, articles that they had collected one summer when they felt they needed to think about how things were connected.

And the other of them, they lost their job a few weeks after the buildings fell, began writing a computer program that they would never finish. They made a program that took all the discussion on the internet that the other of them was looking at all day long in order to build their charts and scrambled it. The program then made a fake page of information where none of the connections, the analysis, the numbers made any sense. The program took hours to make and they would get up in the morning and turn on the computer and start before breakfast. Then they would go and make coffee and return to the computer. This would go on all day and when it started to get dark they would turn on a small lamp that didn't extend much light beyond the desk and they would continue in the light of the small lamp and the light from the monitor of the computer which spread out over the light of the small lamp and filled the room with a certain specific bluish glow. Their shoulders kept getting tighter and tighter as they worked harder and harder to scramble the information that kept being called out by the other in the room below. Because they barely moved from the computer, they often grew stiff from not moving all of their limbs. They were possessed by a special feeling, a feeling that the only escape, the only way out from all the endlessly bad information that came over the television and the internet was to keep scrambling it. And they saw this scrambling as an endless chore, as each day large amounts of new information was produced and this producing of new information continued into the night as they slept.

Eventually the planes stopped crashing in their dreams and their concerns turned from the planes to the air. What was left of the buildings burned on longer than their nightmares, burned for many months. It burned on and on. They continued to watch it billow and feather over the island in the Atlantic on the internet. They continued to be able to smell it in their neighborhood on the other island in the Atlantic. The smoke was cloying, oppressive. It made their stomach turn.

There was obviously poison in it. While breathing it, they would often feel as if they were going to throw up and several times when they were walking down the street they had to lean into the side of a building and just try to breathe, or try to not breathe, or do something to keep from throwing up. Some days were worse than others and they did not realize until many months later that these worse days might have been the days when the twenty-four thousand pounds of freon that was stored beneath the two buildings was burning off.

They talked all day long about the air, trying to figure out how it would impact their body. All they knew at the time was that it was impossible to figure out what was in the air at that time. Various government representatives would get on the news and insist that the air was okay. But how could it be? Breathing made them retch, made all of them retch. Must have even made the government representative retch, although they never saw a government official talk at all about retching. They talked about the air all day long because they wanted to talk about something other than the operations with names like Operation Enduring Freedom, Operation Anaconda, Operation Snipe, Operation Mountain Lion, Operation Mountain Sweep, Operation Mountain Storm, Operation Valiant Strike, Operation Mountain Viper, and Operation Mountain Blizzard that were so obviously sure to happen. They so wanted to talk about air so as not to talk about what was going to happen that they and their friends became air-quality experts with differing opinions. They would meet in a coffee shop and one of them would insist that the air was okay because government officials said so. And then another would point to how it obviously was not okay, how government agencies kept altering their standards to make the air okay. Or they would argue that the air was okay to the government agencies only because they were not testing for what was in the air. Or that each of the substances in the air might be okay on their own but who knew what happened when they were combined. Words like asbestos, lead, mercury, dioxins, furans, hydrogen cyanide, benzene, xylene, chromium, polychlorinated biphenyls, aromatic hydrocarbons, and volatile organic compounds entered their daily conversations.

They felt ill for months. Ill because of breathing. Ill because of what was happening and the operations to come with names like Operation Industrial Sweep, Operation Chamberlain, Operation Sweeney, Operation O.K. Corral, Operation Iron Hammer, Operation Eagle Curtain, Operation All American Tiger, Operation Ivy Cyclone, Operation Ivy Cyclone II, Operation Boothill, and Operation Rifles Blitz. They didn't wear masks like some of them did. Instead they tried to avoid the air. They tried to avoid breathing. It did not work. The air continued to enter their lungs like those operations that continued to be planned without their consent and despite their protest. They could hold off breathing for a few minutes every now and then but then mere seconds later they would be gasping for breath on the street corner.

With the things in the air, the asbestos, lead, mercury, dioxins, furans, hydrogen cyanide, benzene, xylene, chromium, polychlorinated biphenyls, aromatic hydrocarbons, and volatile organic compounds, and the planes, came other flying things, came ghosts. Ghosts entered their bodies with the smoky air. They entered them through their nose and then went down into their lungs and then embedded themselves in their bloodstream where they then traveled throughout their body, even past the blood-brain barrier and deep into some part of their brain, some sensitive part that had no name and that they themselves did not know that they had deep down inside themselves, some part beneath even the gray matter that had told them to move to the island in the Atlantic. These were the same ghosts that had used the air waves and called on cell phones and sent out e-mails and left messages on answering machines right before the buildings fell down.

Everyone breathed the ghosts whether they wanted to or not. There was no avoiding them. Some called out to the ghosts, begged them to come. They put up signs all over the city describing the ghosts, listing their personal details such as a certain green bag that the ghost had carried when last seen or a certain bulky white sweater or a leather jacket that the ghost was wearing when the buildings fell down. The signs urged the ghosts to use the airwaves and call. But the ghosts didn't call or they couldn't call or perhaps it was that the way that they called was to enter the bodies of those who still had bodies and do their work there, changing the brain chemistry of those who remained dependent on breathing in and out because they still had bodies. Some of those who breathed in the ghosts had trouble breathing. Some kept getting sick. Some took to twitching as if the ghosts had embedded themselves in the part of the gray matter of their brain that controlled their reflexes and their muscles. Others just felt the ghosts inside and went on living with them because they knew that was just what happened sometimes, sometimes ghosts came and lived with them.

The air was not only full of the ghosts and full of chemicals in combinations never before seen, but it was also full of fear and it was full of bigotry. And then when not full of bigotry, it was full of judgments. Everyone was breathing these emotions in and out all day long and retching on them also. For a long time they didn't want to talk to other people in the city because they felt like they couldn't trust what they might say. When they brought up the people who ran the planes into the building, they usually ducked out of the conversation. They hated to go into bars because there was often some drunk talking about killing everyone in some part of the world far away that was being blamed for the buildings falling down by some government official. Because of all of this, the public space was suddenly a disorientating spin. Suddenly, as in a musical where everyone in unison begins an elaborately synchronized dance, shops on the island in the Atlantic taped posters in the shape of the flag of the government that currently occupied the continent to their windows up and down the block, buckets of flag magnets were placed for impulse buys beside cash registers, taxis began to each have their own flag bumper sticker, businesspeople wore flag pins in their lapels or pinned their scarves together with flag stickpins, teenagers sewed flag patches on their backpacks and some wore flag earrings, babies were dressed in flag onesies and they flinched a little as flag stocking caps were put on their heads but gave in once they recognized the warmth, the bank gave away flag checks and flag pens in exchange for customer accounts, the post office sold new design after new design of flag stamps, and there were ads on the television about flags that had holders that attached to car windows so that flags might flutter in the wind as the car drove. There were suddenly so many flags in so many places that they who refused flags on principle, who had even tried to not buy flag stamps if possible for years, became nervous that their refusal of the flag would make them vulnerable, that the flag wearers would notice and come after them. And they talked with their friends about the flags and whether they should put a flag on some part of them also. And they talked about their confusion around the flag. They recognized that the flag symbolized all those who died when the airplanes went into the buildings, but their brain made them purposely naïve as it refused to understand how this happened. Their brain refused to understand the voodoo of symbol making where distress about the dead turned into a desire to wear a flag pin somewhere and have it mean that they supported the government that currently occupied the continent.

Their brain refused to understand many things. It refused to understand the language that those around them used. Or that the media used. It refused to understand what was terror and what was war. It refused separations between just wars and unjust wars, bombs and smart bombs, deterrence and self-defense. They felt the use of these words in their bodies as a spasm-inducing linguistic trick. Their stomach would twist and gurgle anytime these words were used. They would hear the word terrorist and their chest would tighten across their breastbones. They would read the words just wars or smart bombs and their bowels would twist. Their brain refused to understand how violence had made things different. How it redrew maps and changed their vocabulary. How it changed their aesthetics and morals and emotions. It refused to understand why violence led to new violence and not to a rejection of violence.

Their brain could admit that a wound had been made, a big, open, bleeding wound that was starting to fester. They felt this wound themselves in their own body. But their brain refused to understand why the emphasis wasn't on healing the wound, why the government that currently occupied the continent let the wound become feverish and swollen and leaking and then once it was all feverish and swollen and leaking deliberately rubbed dirt in it.

They could understand the desire for the newspaper to write a paragraph-long obituary on everyone who died when floor after floor of the buildings went crashing down. They had died, and in their culture the dead got written up in the newspaper. But their brain refused to understand why the same newspaper accepted it a few months later when the government that currently occupied the continent refused to let them show photographs of their own dead who died while trying to kill them of another place. And it refused to understand why any newspaper tolerated it when the government that currently occupied the continent refused to let them show photographs of those that were killed in the places that the government that currently occupied the continent bombed in retribution for the fallen buildings. For months during the wars that came out of the fallen buildings, they looked on the internet just for the names of the dead of these places, just for a list of names. They felt that if they could find a list of the names of the dead of the other places they could maybe understand something. They did not know what. But for some reason the list of names felt crucial, felt as if it were an obligation, part of being human. So they searched and they searched, compulsively clicking, trying search term after search term. But they could not find a list anywhere. They wondered if this list was out there but in a language other than the expansionist language they spoke, out there somewhere for someone who could read differently than they could.

Basically, language itself became impossible. It was no longer that it was expansionist and carried expansionist values in it, but it made no sense. Government officials were speaking to them in a sort of blather that their brain refused to let into their ears as sense. Even though they were trained in the analysis of the expansionist language and its structures, trained in close reading, trained in making sense out of nonsense, trained in interpreting the old ways of the avant-garde, trained in making meaning out of works that used fragmentation, quotation, disruption, disjunction, agrammatical syntax, and so on, they refused the sense. They abandoned their old tools of analysis. There was an argument made by many poets at the time that because the government that currently occupied the continent spoke in clear, smooth language and always lied, it was wrong to use clear language, thus these poets had chosen to do their writing with fragmentation, quotation, disruption, disjunction, agrammatical syntax, and so on. But with this war, all the government officials avoided clear language and stuttered. Instead of speaking in a smooth clear language, and despite their having an elite heritage and having attended elite schools where they were well trained in the standards of the expansionist language, they spoke mainly in fragmentation, quotation, disruption, disjunction, agrammatical syntax, and so on. It was as if the government that currently occupied the continent had taken over one of the few remaining tools of resistance, the very small tools of fragmentation, quotation, disruption, disjunction, agrammatical syntax, and so on, and even used them, leaving not only the poets but also the organizers and the activists empty handed.

It was not just the expansionist language as spoken by the government that currently occupied the continent that they refused to understand. They refused to understand what was happening locally. There was a constant slide between what was true and what was false. It was not only a time of ghosts but a time of endless fake bomb threats. Frequently in this time after the buildings fell and before Halloween they would walk down the street and see people standing around outside a building because someone had called in a bomb threat there. There were never bombs, just threats. One of them had gone to the smaller and more populated island in the Atlantic the day after the buildings fell and they had walked from their workplace to the middle of the island and as they walked they had several times seen people running out of buildings in response to some bomb threat or other. This continued for some time. There were so many bomb threats on the subway for months after the buildings fell that it became impossible to get anywhere. Subway cars were constantly stopped or were rerouted or were taken off duty. Once the subway that they were on stopped between stations for half an hour. Everyone waited calmly but after fifteen minutes a woman in the car began crying with anxiety. Their anxiety took over the car and others joined in the crying. Much of the car began crying and they themselves began twitching. Then suddenly the car began moving. There was no explanation for the stop. The car just continued on and the people who had been crying with anxiety stopped crying and got on and off as usual. Regularly, the subway car would pull into a station and never leave. Another subway car would come in the wrong direction and they would get on it just to get away from the stopped subway car, which they always felt had to be a sign of something bad on the car or ahead of the car or in the tunnel or in the station. The trick, they felt, and others seemed to join them in this, was just to keep moving. To get off one subway train and then get on another, even if it went in totally the wrong direction. If they just kept moving perhaps they would be moving away from the unarticulated bad things that may or may not happen.

It was not just they who were confused. One friend called them up and said their partner, usually a fine if mundane partner, kept talking about the importance of bombing someone, anyone, in response, and they didn't know what to do, should they break up with them or would it pass? Another friend went the other way and anytime there was anyone on the television who was mourning someone lost in the buildings they would go into a tirade about how they especially deserved it because all the citizens of the government that currently occupied the continent deserved it, how they themselves deserved it, and those who worked in the financial industry deserved it even more. And then with people they trusted, the people they wanted to talk about things with, they didn't know what to say really. They would meet them for a cup of coffee or tea and talk but they could only talk meaninglessly about the walk they took last week where they went around the park instead of through it. Or they would talk about the itchiness of their dry skin, which was caused by the forced-air heat. Or they would talk about other people, about who had a cold or who had a sore throat or who had a nosebleed or who had a cough or who was having difficulty breathing. They did not mention the ghosts.

Instead they continued to talk about the air. They continued to talk in great detail about the asbestos, lead, mercury, dioxins, furans, hydrogen cyanide, benzene, xylene, chromium, polychlorinated biphenyls, aromatic hydrocarbons, and volatile organic compounds in the air, about the two hundred thousand gallons of diesel fuel and transformer oils leaking beneath the burning buildings. Then they talked again about how government officials kept adjusting the tolerable levels of various substances upward. They talked about their worries that the workers cleaning debris from the site were all likely to get sick again in another six years from the air. All this talk about breath and throat and air continued to be a coded way to talk about the fallen buildings and not mention their confusions, their inability to escape the ghosts. They didn't know what to say to their friend with the suddenly war-mongering partner. Instead they changed the subject and joked about how they were going to turn into one of those girls in the middle of the continent who all together developed a sort of rash that was probably caused by some sort of sympathetic stress in reaction to the buildings falling down.

For years they had watched the television news and then a mildly funny late-night talk show before they went to sleep at night because both were boring and put them to sleep. But both of these programs went from boring soporific to horrifying. The talk show suddenly had those in the military that currently occupied the continent doing its top-ten lists. There were endless jokes about how people who lived in the area that extends from the eastern Mediterranean Sea to the Persian Gulf dressed or what they ate or how they treated their women. One day the news showed turkey vultures at the edge of the site where the buildings fell down. Another time a forensic pathologist had a pile of dust from the site and they sprayed the dust with a substance that would glow in the presence of DNA and then proceeded to make the pile of dust they took from the site glow in order to demonstrate that they were all breathing in DNA all day long. On yet another day, hacking children with aggravated asthma filled the screen. On yet another, people who suddenly began getting nosebleeds were testifying. Once, the group of girls from the middle of the continent who claimed to be getting rashes were featured with the doctors who theorized that the rashes were psychosomatic. They would look at the newspaper on the internet and notice stories about anthrax and then stories about other fallen planes nearby and then stories about a government official who was claiming to have prevented a dirty bomb from exploding. The news was full of rumors of attacks that might happen tomorrow or the next day or some time next week or just sometime in some undefined future. One day it would be an especially beautiful bridge that connected the islands on the Atlantic that was going to be bombed. Then a statue that represented liberty the next. Then suddenly the news would say that all apartment buildings are at risk. Then an especially beautiful bridge on the other side of the continent. Then the city where the government that currently occupied the continent was located. Then the cycle would start again. An especially beautiful bridge that connected the islands on the Atlantic, a statue that represented liberty the next, all apartment buildings, an especially beautiful bridge on the other side of the continent, the city where the government that currently occupied the continent was located . . . None of them took the news at all seriously. How could they? One day it told them to stay in their apartment and the next day it told them that their apartment was unsafe.

Whether any of this was true or not they did not know as they no longer believed anything really. But when they read that the dirty bomb was not targeted at their island but at the city where the government that currently occupied the continent was located they had to admit that they felt relief. But this relief made no more sense than the news with its endless stories about suicide bombs, but never anything about the reasons why the suicide bombs were happening. When they watched the news, they could easily think that people were spontaneously blowing themselves up for no reason. The news often showed a mother in another place saying that they would love for their son to martyr themselves by blowing themselves and others from their place up, but without the history of occupations and analysis of women's roles in the family in this other place, it was just pure horror. The news about anthrax made no sense, never made any sense. The anthrax was a strain from a lab on the continent but it was never clear if it represented an internal or an external threat. In their search for analysis, in their search to understand mothers willing to martyr their sons as something other than pure horror, they often turned to the internet late at night, when they couldn't sleep. They read e-mail discussion lists and listened to those with greater confidence than themselves proclaim. They read the alternative press. They read the press from other places. If it was in the expansionist language, they searched it down. They read and they read. They read so much that their minds got blurry and they couldn't remember the source of anything. They could no longer distinguish between what was said by teenagers in their blogs and what was said by someone with a long history of astute analysis. It was impossible to figure out what was going on anywhere. All they could figure out with any certainty was that the reason the buildings had collapsed had something to do with groups of theys on both sides having trouble thinking about theys on the side they were not on.

As it was a time when words like asbestos, lead, mercury, dioxins, furans, hydrogen cyanide, benzene, xylene, chromium, polychlorinated biphenyls, aromatic hydrocarbons, and volatile organic compounds entered their daily conversations, a time of ghosts, a time of endless flags, a time of bigoted statements, a time of various operations already happening and operations to come with names like Operation Rifle Sweep, Operation Bayonet Lightning, Operation Bulldog Mammoth, Operation Clear Area, Operation Abilene, Operation Panther Squeeze, Operation Red Dawn, Operation Panther Backroads, Operation Ivy Blizzard, Operation Arrowhead Blizzard, and Operation Iron Justice, it was also a time for endless memorials. It was a time when other places, usually places indebted to the government that currently occupied the continent, a very rich government that often loaned money to other poorer governments on draconian terms, took out advertisements in the newspapers and magazines of the city sending their condolences. Some cities and some unusually rich individuals offered money. Other places sent things. The city accepted some of these gifts and refused others. The city of Stuttgart sent over daffodil bulbs and the city accepted the bulbs and the bulbs were planted all over the city streets, in the little patches of dirt that surrounded the trees. These daffodils would bloom in the first weeks of April but a week later when the temperature freakishly went up to ninety degrees they all died suddenly.

In March, the city installed a memorial that was two shafts of light pointing up into the sky. The light was made by two banks of forty-four searchlights. They tended not to like memorials or monuments. Public mourning weirded them out. It had bad politics most of the time. It used sentiment to cover over deeper histories. It was all about nation. It so rarely had more than one side to it. They had refused to go to memorials or monuments ever since that summer after second grade when their mother took them to the great lawn in the city where the government that currently occupied the continent was located. Then they had taken an antimemorial stand out of boredom. But as they got older, they politicized their boredom. They even read books and articles on monuments to justify their distaste. At moments, once they got sufficiently theorized, they tried to think their way through this by thinking about Antigone and the public need to bury a body. But the minute they thought this, they then realized that Antigone was a figure of resistance against the state, not the state putting up one more piece of art to support its endless and unjustified killing of people of other places as well as its endless and unjust killing of a disproportionate number of its own people of certain races and classes in the pursuit of endless and unjustified killing of people in other places.

The towers-of-light memorial was there all the time. They couldn't refuse to leave the car and miss out on it as they had as a teenager. At first this inability to refuse the towers-of-light annoyed them. Then months passed and they found themselves relying on the towers-of-light to orientate themselves in the grid of the island, just as they had used the actual towers. And then, even worse they found themselves mesmerized against their will by the towers-of-light. They told themselves that this was okay because these towers-of-light weren't memorializing people whom the military that currently occupied the continent had killed in other places or had sent off to kill and be killed. They were instead reminders of a building. They meant only that buildings had once been there and because they were just shafts of light they didn't necessarily have to blame anyone or tell stories of patriotism. They were the opposite of that staged image of the firefighters raising the flag. And they were also the opposite of that other horribly moving image of the five firemen carrying out the priest from the rubble. They tried to convince themselves that even though they had emotions, the towers-of-light did not necessarily require sentiment or patriotism. They knew this was not true. That the towers-of-light carried those terms such as wars and unjust wars, bombs and smart bombs, deterrence and self-defense as anything, as everything, else around them did. But still they found themselves often standing in the middle of the sidewalk at night mesmerized by the clouds, which otherwise couldn't be seen in the dark night sky, caught in the light. There was something about seeing the clouds in the light that was indescribably beautiful to them. The towers-of-light illuminated what was going on unseen in the dark sky. They illuminated the ghosts that were still floating over the city six months later. The moon would go through the lights also and sometimes it looked as if the lights were pointing all who wanted to look away from what was going on around them—the words like asbestos, lead, mercury, dioxins, furans, hydrogen cyanide, benzene, xylene, chromium, polychlorinated biphenyls, aromatic hydrocarbons, and volatile organic compounds that entered their daily conversations, the ghosts, the endless flags, the bigoted statements, the various operations already happening and operations to come with names like Operation Rifles Fury, Operation Salm, Operation Devil Siphon, Operation Iron Grip, Operation Iron Force, Operation Choke Hold, Operation Warhorse Whirlwind, Operation Iron Resolve, Operation Market Sweep, Operation Saloon, and Operation Rock Slide—off towards the moon, a place without all of this, or so they hoped.

8

Time passed. The towers-of-light searchlights were taken down and they stopped looking for the buildings to orientate themselves when they were lost. They and their reflexes forgot about the buildings. They had read an article about how the buildings had been so tall they were in the traditional flight path of sparrows, black-eyed juncos, woodcocks, and brown creepers, and because the birds got easily confused by the glass and the lights on the building they had often flown into the buildings when the buildings where there. People would meet on the weekends just to gather up the corpses and to count the dead and then they would post photographs of the dead on a website. They found around a thousand a year. After they read this, they hoped that just as they forgot to look for the buildings to figure out what direction was north or south that the thousand birds who might have died year after year also forgot about the buildings and resumed their flight paths. And this thought of the collectivity of birds resuming their flight paths, assuming that their path was hardwired into them, dumbly comforted them.

And then after the buildings fell down, it felt not only as if all those things that made them love the city, all that touching all day long, all those neighborhoods famous for what was often called alternative lifestyles, all that poetry written in the name of eros and neighborhood, all those languages in line at the post office, all that had seduced them to the city in the first place was under attack, but also everyone they knew ended up unemployed. One of them had no job to lose because they were trying to leave their job at the university on the island in the middle of the Pacific and had not been able to find another one. One of them lost their job a few weeks after the buildings fell. One of them kept their job and supported the other of them. Among their friends, a few kept their jobs for four or five months longer than the others but then in most instances they too lost theirs.

This losing of jobs happened in waves. It was as if companies decided together to use the fallen buildings as an excuse to get rid of everyone they could because they realized that it would appear as if it were inevitable if they all did it around the same time. They and their friends were used to being barely employed so life went on as usual but with everyone making weekly calls to a machine at the unemployment office and then using push buttons on their phone to request their check and no one being all that upset about it and many feeling glad that they no longer had to go to whatever job they had. They all just did their writing at their desks at home instead of doing it between tasks at their jobs. They went without health insurance but they had done this before. And the truth of the matter was that where they lived there was so much money, there was more money concentrated there than in most of the places on the globe, that they did all right. They had fewer drinks at the bar. And they worried some about paying their rent and maybe if they had saved up some money they might have to spend some of it or they might have to borrow from a parent or a brother or a sister. But no one went hungry. No one lost their apartment. Some of them were rich and it didn't really matter. Some of them had parents who had money so they knew they had money coming to them at some point in their lives even if they didn't have it in their pockets now. But most of them came from working-class families, some from small rural towns in the middle of the continent, towns without libraries and bookstores, and even though they didn't have any money coming to them from these families they knew that there was enough money in the city that they could live easily. Things might get bad for them fifty years from now when they couldn't really work and didn't really have any retirement but they didn't worry much about that now.

So in their home, only one of them worked and the other two got by with freelance or temp jobs every once in a while. They didn't have a lot of extra money, but they were able to pay the rent every month easily and then they also went out to eat several nights a week and cooked food that was high in protein in their home and they drank wines in the ten-dollar range and they had the possibility of future income and so were not that worried. In general things went on as usual in their home, just with fewer of them working and with words like asbestos, lead, mercury, dioxins, furans, hydrogen cyanide, benzene, xylene, chromium, polychlorinated biphenyls, aromatic hydrocarbons, and volatile organic compounds in their daily conversations, and with the various operations already happening and operations to come with names like Operation Final Cut, Operation Saber Turner II, Operation Tomahawk, Operation Trailblazer, Operation Eagle Liberty 3, Operation Devil Clinch, Operation Rocketman, Operation Iron Promise, and Operation Shillelagh constantly in their thoughts.

Comfort became a strange emotion that they desired even as it constantly eluded them. They read in the paper that the fallen buildings caused people to fall in love, to make babies, to give rings to one another, to settle down finally after years of having trouble with commitments. And they themselves went that year to many elaborate weddings. They went to weddings for friends who were obviously going to get married at some point because they were the sort to get married and because they loved people who were of the opposite gender and were thus allowed to get married by the government that currently occupied the continent. But they also went to weddings for friends who had for years been involved with people of their same gender and thus not allowed to get married by the government that currently occupied the continent or for friends who had seemed not the marrying type because they often changed partners. They did not want to make too much of all this desire for government-sanctioned coupling, but still the world felt as if it was becoming even more defined by conventional models of family, as if even their friends, friends they had chosen because they were not the sort to buy into conventional models of family, woke up one morning and suddenly said to themselves that conventional models of family were for them and began to act accordingly. It was as if a ring of fire were burning even more brightly than it usually did. As if a ring of fire, a ring that they realized had been burning steady for some time, suddenly flared up and this flare might burn them.

They loved their friends and they wanted them to love each other and they were always willing to go to even a government-sanctioned celebration of love even if they felt that the institution was flawed as long as the government that currently occupied the continent said who could and could not get married and even though they were always torn between the position that no one should get married or everyone should just get married over and over indiscriminately until the government that currently occupied the continent left people's commitments alone. But still the more weddings they attended, the more nervous they became about being called a pervert, even though they enjoyed the fancy white dresses with beading and they liked the taste of the cakes with overly optimistic and sweet icing and the plastic male and female figures on the top and they danced with abandon when the d.j. spun songs for dancing. They did not worry that their friends would call them a pervert. Although they realized that some might and they felt as if they should be able to do this if they wanted to and they should not overreact to it. They realized that for the most part their friends would think that it was overstatement or a joke for them to call themselves perverts. Still their worry that the government that currently occupied the continent might notice them and call them a pervert was so scary that it made them want to pull down all the shades on their apartment and not let anyone know that three of them lived there.

They had raw skin that was easily chafed by the way relationships got represented in the things they read. In their hypersensitivity, they embraced the word pervert when really it was probably an overstatement and the fact that they felt that everything was a metaphor against them did not mean that they were that abnormal, that unacceptable. They had been hypersensitive for years. When they read love poems that took the love between a man and a woman as a given and as singular, they complained. Again and again they had made students on the island in the middle of the Pacific rewrite their poems so that the genders and numbers of partners were not obvious and obviously coupled, as if rewriting student love poems would solve anything. When they saw that their colleague assigned an anthology to their students that included an essay about the disgust the author felt for their in-law who was a follower of a religion that allowed them to have more than one partner, they complained to them about the book, and when their colleague with an amused look on their faces said they were not using that essay, just the other essays in the book, they still got upset that they would require students to purchase a book with such an essay in it. And they continued to hold onto this hypersensitivity when they moved to the island in the Atlantic. When the same newspaper that had said that the fallen buildings made people fall in love, make babies, give rings to one another, settle down finally after years of having trouble with commitments published an editorial defending the kidnapping of a child from parents who were followers of a religion that allowed them to have more than one partner, they stopped reading the opinion pages of the newspaper. When the elderly lefty poet read their poems that compared imperialism to perversion and suggested that having more than one partner and sleeping around was analogous to using too much fossil fuel, the next day they lectured friends who had liked the reading and told them that they should think more about who gets excluded from anti-imperial struggle as if their liking the poem had high stakes in the anti-imperial struggle. When a literary theorist from the continent across the Atlantic known for their explorations of jouissance claimed in an interview that those who questioned the convention of the coupled relationship ended up in therapy all confused years later they stopped reading their work and refused to quote it in any articles even though they had admired their work's complicated feminism for many years.

Their analysis had no subtlety. They refused to distinguish between their situation and that of those who were members of various religions that let one gender marry more than once but not the other gender. They were very annoyed when students said that their love poems were autobiographical and they could not multiply or ambiguate the lovers as a result. And yet just as they were overly sensitive and saw themselves in every essay, in every poem, they also did the opposite and had trouble fitting themselves into theories where they might have fit. They refused the word queer to describe themselves and they told themselves that they did this out of respect because they were not sexually involved with people of the same gender. They felt that queer needed to not include everything if it was to have any meaning and they wanted queer to have meaning. And they were suspicious of queer because they knew so many who lived their lives in ways that looked like for all intents and purposes as if they were indulging in conventional models of family who would claim to be queer. It was a fashionable thing to do among the people they went to graduate school with in the nineties. And so when a colleague had once said in a faculty meeting that they should teach the queer studies course until the department hired someone who was involved with someone of the same gender, they expressed puzzlement and a slight annoyance rather than enthusiasm.

Around this time a major literary theorist whose work had changed their thinking in profound ways, whose work had made discussions of variabilities of genders and sexualities part of expansionist language departments, held a talk. The theorist was especially popular because they had written a groundbreaking work about how gender was more socially constructed than anything else and many people felt close to them because of their work. Their work had a smartness and a hipness and was read by a certain class of student, a certain well-dressed and highly fluent class of student. The theorist tended to not be as well dressed as those who came to hear them. They had a certain down-to-earthness about them despite the notorious difficulty of their work. This down-to-earthness took the form of practical dress, an undistinguished haircut, and a certain way of standing where their head jutted forward and their shoulders back. While much of their work was about gesture and flounce, the markers of excess and exaggeration that make gender, markers that were so well reconfigured in their followers, they avoided all gesture and flounce. Their talk was about the importance of queer theory after the buildings fell down. They argued against mourning and complained about those daily obituaries that the newspaper was running about each person who had died when the buildings fell down. They liked the talk. They themselves were concerned about how to deal with their own sense of mourning and how to keep it separate from the endless patriotism around them. They had trouble understanding those obituaries with their emphasis on the normalcy of the deads' lives. And similarly, even though they were now comforted by the idea that the birds could resume their migratory paths now that the buildings had fallen, they had trouble understanding those endless photographs of the dead birds who had run into the buildings when the buildings were still there in a time in which they could not even get a decent count of the dead of other nations. At the end of the talk the theorist spoke some along a queer-theory-now-more-than-ever theme. And it was this that confused them. Queer theory they felt had been so little help with helping them think about western economic privilege and had been only of the most provisional help with thinking about polygamy, about those cultures of polygamy that existed in both the continent where they lived and the area that extends from the eastern Mediterranean Sea to the Persian Gulf. This is where they got lost yet again.

Once a friend of theirs who had surgically changed their gender asked them why they did not speak more publicly and explicitly about their relationship. The implication behind their comment was that perhaps they were more in the closet, even though their friend did not suggest what they should come out as. When their friend asked them this they immediately felt guilty and wondered at the same time if the reason they did not come out was that they saw themselves more as perverts than as anything radical.

The guilt that their friend's question caused reminded them of how they'd never complained about a poem that they had heard read over and over when they lived on the island in the middle of the Pacific that compared colonialism to getting fucked in the ass. And then, the poem went: getting fucked in the ass is supposed to be a turn on—Get real! And it continued: Whoever thought that crap up deserves to get whacked. Every time they heard this poem read, and they heard it many times because the literary culture of the island in the middle of the Pacific tended to have the same people reading over and over, they left the reading feeling angry at themselves for not standing up and saying that they hated colonialism but they thought getting fucked in the ass was a turn on. They justified their silence by telling themselves that another continental haole did not need to stand up and yet again harass a poet who had genealogical ties to the island from before the whaling ships arrived, that their role teaching in the complex was already an affront to poets who had genealogical ties to the island from before the whaling ships arrived and why keep adding to it, why keep playing the haole schoolteacher? They tried, in other words, like many others, to justify their inaction by arguing that race should trump sexuality. But really they did not stand up at the readings and say they thought getting fucked in the ass was a turn on because they already felt like a pervert, not like a strident and political queer, and they were weak and a little ashamed, or perhaps it was embarrassed, and didn't want to draw any more attention to their perversion as a result.

Their friend's question also reminded them of their reaction to the polyamorous potluck that another friend kept insisting they attend when they lived on the island in the middle of the Pacific. At first they had said no way to their friend's repeated invitation. And then they had given in under the constant pressure of their friend. Actually they had agreed to go to the polyamorous potluck so as to get their friend to stop asking them to go to the orgy. Next to the orgy, the potluck seemed safe. The polyamorous potluck was held by a group that called themselves the Pali Pals, a cute pun as pali means mountain in the language that was on the island in the middle of the Pacific before the whaling ships arrived. They joked among themselves that they were going to the polyamorous potluck because they thought it would be something they could make fun of with their friends, their friends who were not polyamorous. They went, basically, with a plan to indulge in a mild version of self-hatred that would allow them to join their friends in making fun of them. There were about twenty people at the potluck. They were of different ages although most of them were haoles. They quickly realized that all the Pali Pals lived in sets of two and then they invited other Pali Pals into their beds in various configurations. Faced with a room full of fellow perverts, they were full of scorn. They told themselves it was just a swingers club, while they were the real perverts because they lived together, moving from bed to bed, sharing meals and chores. They stayed at the potluck only half an hour and then fled, giggling nervously and mocking themselves, telling themselves that they were not cut out to be polyamorous. They were instead just amorous.

And they also thought in response to their friend's question, how they resorted to secrecy about their personal life when meeting new people, like when they took a Spanish course. When they signed up for the Spanish course they joked that they were taking a Spanish course so that they could move south when the military that currently occupied the continent on which they lived began bombing one more place. They said that the places to the south loved poets so they would be fine there. But really they took the Spanish course so as not to feel as if they were from a working-class family, from a small rural town in the middle of the continent, a town without libraries and bookstores, so they could maybe feel less slump shouldered at academic talks. In Spanish class they had to answer mundane personal questions about themselves. And in this class they suddenly became someone who was married. The teacher would ask ¿Usted valora fidelidad? and they would answer sí. They described their partner in the singular, as a tall and bald writer of books for teenagers. They told a Spanish version of their life where their rings of fire merged into one ring. In Spanish class they not only valued fidelity, but they lived in a home with a small cat and they went to the movies on the weekends and watched the news on week nights. They stayed home a lot in their Spanish class life. They liked to cook and go to bed early. And their Spanish class life had no switching between beds. And, they claimed, they enjoyed this life.

Eventually they just gave up. Or sort of gave up. They had to confess that they kept going to movies that had threesomes just so they could complain some more about them to their friends with a slightly pious and aggrieved tone about how they all ended in suicide or in the duality being reestablished as if they were romantic comedies. And when they sometimes met others who also configured themselves in three, they longed to ask them things, like did they too have a schedule for who slept in what bed? What did they do about those awkward moments when colleagues invited them and their partner to dinner? Did they too have a rule that made them have to mumble something about having more than one partner and could all of them come? What did they do when they wrote their name plus two on the office sign up sheet for the holiday party and then got an e-mail from the secretary that roommates were not invited, only spouses? Did they too have a chore wheel where the wheel was cut into three wedges? But usually they were too shy. And they avoided becoming friends with these others like them as if people would make even more fun of them if they saw them with others like them.

So they had to admit that the real answer to their friend who had changed genders was that they did not come out more because they were weak. They admired their friend for their ability to walk into a room fully and strikingly as what they were but they could not claim this for themselves at this time. They were stupidly afraid in a way that made no sense but that entered their body without their permission. They were now afraid to walk home late at night because they worried people knew they were a pervert. How anyone would know, they did not know. Even if they had wanted to somehow act or dress in a way that made it clear to those around them that they were perverts, there was no clear and obvious way to do this. But still they worried, as if they were a schoolgirl with a new crush, that people knew. It was absurd to say that they felt unsafe not because of the fallen buildings but because of the government-sanctioned weddings and conventional models of family and personal essays in the newspaper, but that is how it felt to them. Or perhaps it wasn't the weddings per se but perhaps it was that some part of their body was listening when a well-known televangelist blamed the fallen buildings on the pagans and the abortionists and the feminists and the gays and the lesbians and the ACLU and the People for the American Way and they transferred statements like this into a slightly legitimate unsafe feeling and used government-sanctioned weddings as an excuse because of sloppy thinking, because it was easier, closer to hand, and thinking it was the fault of government-sanctioned weddings made it all a little less scary.

Before the buildings had fallen down they made it a point not to feel unsafe because they felt that unsafe feelings were created by the media, by an often racist and sexist media. To feel unsafe was to be racist. To feel safe was to be antiracist. They justified this other form of somewhat sloppy thinking in their heads by thinking a lot about their white privilege. But after the buildings fell down they felt unsafe and no racial analysis could help. None of this was rational. And they knew it was hubris to think everyone was against them and their tiny lives. And it probably wasn't really the fear of physical harm by an unknown imaginary squad of moral people that worried them. But there was no denying that they felt as if the cloud of smoke that came from the still-burning remains of the fallen buildings was a cloud that was heavy and thick with fear and conservative values, so heavy and thick that they could not see with any distance or depth, could not float through it and above it, so heavy and thick that they were held down by the cloud and all they could see were vague and menacing shapes that they suspected were armed versions of fear and conservative values with shoot-to-kill orders.

They tried to balance out all their anxiety with loud celebrations of life. They tried to do this in often ineffectual ways. They might make out in public while standing in line at the grocery or stay out late chatting happily in a dark smoky room drinking with friends who were not at home planning their government-sanctioned marriages or maybe they would just go home and smoke some pot and lie on their bed watching television and think about how soft the bed can feel at moments, how deep it would let them enter, or they might talk loudly and excitedly with each other about the latest summer blockbuster movie or the latest book of literary theory that used sociological methods to show the conflicts between urban and rural spaces in the novel as if that really mattered to them. And they could live with the sudden realization that it was a new conservative time because they had things like intoxication and movies and books that let them be preoccupied with other concerns.

While the collapsing buildings did not cause them to fall in love, make babies, give rings to one another, settle down finally after years of having trouble with commitments, the collapsing buildings did provoke an unusual number of poetry readings and gatherings. At the poetry readings, poets suddenly only had two choices: to read poems about the buildings collapsing or to not read poems about the buildings collapsing. Most of the poets who read in the time that followed the buildings collapsing read poems about the buildings collapsing. The poems they read were still full of fragmentation, quotation, disruption, disjunction, and agrammatical syntax, and so on, but they used these tools to talk about the buildings collapsing. One poet read a poem where they listed all the office equipment that they had seen collected at a dump site for the buildings after they collapsed. Another poet read an especially moving and spare poem that was a long list of nouns, each noun surrounded by a repeated phrase so that the poem went these words are the only words, this day is the only day and on and on for one hundred and twenty-two stanzas. The poem ended with a final stanza of but no one is absent no one is absent anymore. This poem was moving because it reminded them that no relationship is hermetically sealed, that they cannot separate themselves from they who exist at the imposed borders of the national or the personal. It reminded them that pain forms political, public communities in which no one is absent, not even the dead.

But many poets read poems where they did not mention the buildings collapsing and they found these to also be provocative comments about the buildings collapsing because during this time to not mention the buildings was to also mention the buildings. One poet read a poem in five parts and in each part they used only one vowel sound and thus wrote a witty, playful poem. Other poets read poems that they had created by entering a term into an internet search engine and then they would edit a poem out of the language that the search engine returned. The poems written this way were deliberately crass and often sounded angry and racist and sexist but the poets as a group insisted that these poems were about their anger at racist and sexist language, which felt as if it was at an all-time high after the buildings collapsed.

While many things that they heard read at a poetry reading felt moving to them in this time, just as many things felt confusing to them. Once they went to a poetry reading where the poet read from a piece in which they recorded all their conversation for a week and then transcribed it. The poet had picked out to read, they assumed with a certain irony but they didn't know for sure, two passages from their conversations for the week. One was a moment where they told a story about how they had bought an expensive suit and had to have it tailored and they had taken it to the immigrant tailor and then they realized that the immigrant tailor wouldn't understand the cut of the expensive suit so they went to the immigrant tailor's shop first thing in the morning and started pounding on their door so they could get the suit back before the immigrant tailor would begin work and cut it and ruin it. The other was a transcript of a scene at a gathering where the poet retold how someone's partner, the partner was someone whom some people in the room knew, complained about them not being able to get it up in bed. The reading was a dramatic avoidance of talking about the buildings collapsing, as if instead of talking about the buildings collapsing, the poet had chosen to talk about themselves in an unflattering light. It was strange to hear such relentless self-examination at such a time in a room near the still-burning site where the buildings had once been. And that at least two people in the audience were wearing masks because the air was so bad that day made the event even more confusing to them. After the reading they asked one of the masked audience members what they thought of the way the poet decided not to talk about the collapsing buildings but they could not understand the answer because the mask muffled the reply.

After each of these readings, the audience and the poet would all walk together to a bar if the reading was not held at a bar or if the reading had been held at a bar they just stayed there drinking and they would talk about poetry. They talked frequently about the decision the poet who had read made about whether to talk or not talk about the buildings collapsing. They talked about whether it was more of a cliché to talk about the buildings or more of a cliché to not talk about the buildings. They debated whether lyric had any use anymore or if it was a time in which a list of office equipment was more poignant than any well-wrought poem. They debated the relation between poetry and violence and the sudden relevance of poetry about violence. And they talked about poetry that did not have anything to say about violence or the buildings collapsing and yet still felt disturbingly relevant. While they talked they debated whether poetry was a disorientation, that old-fashioned derangement of the senses, or a genre that could be shaped out of facts. And so they also debated whether poetry could be a genre that was for everyone when it was read by so few. And they debated what was innovative and what was not. And what confronted them and what awakened them. They took this poetry that was read to a room of maybe fifty people all sitting in chairs in a badly lit church social room or in a high-end art gallery or in a smoky bar overly seriously. They did this because they saw poetry as a way to think about the linguistic imprecision that so defined their life after the buildings collapsed. And it was by endlessly discussing their minute differences of opinion that they formed themselves into a somewhat cohesive yet permeable social scene.

At the gatherings, their talk was less focused than the talk at the bar after the readings. They still talked about the sorts of things that they usually talked about, but moved more quickly from one idea to the next. They might begin with talk about the complicated personality of poets and how they don't tip at restaurants. And then move to how they were thinking about quitting smoking because of the air or how they were taking up smoking because of the air or how they were smoking more pot because of the air or how they were smoking less pot because of the air and the paranoia that came with the air. Then they might move on to song lyrics and how the words to Brandy sometimes made them cry because of how the song proclaimed a love of a wayward life, a life that they wished they had or a life that they felt they were trying to have. Then next they would skip to talk about the signs in the subway that urged the residents of the city to get grief counseling. Back again to the lyrics of certain pop songs and how these songs were so much more moving than the complicated rhythmic patterns that were used in those poems published in certain journals associated with creative writing programs in the middle of the continent. And then to how they couldn't find a therapist with an opening for the life of them. And then next about whether, when a certain singer sang out I am, I said, if it was a statement of male assertion and privilege or if it was a statement of the emptiness of male assertion and a critique of male privilege. And then they articulated their absurd anger that the television no longer had the reception that it had before the buildings fell and how while the fallen buildings left them numb, minutia and irrelevant details like the bad television reception left them outraged. Next moving to talk about friends who were in relationships who had affairs and when their partners found out they blamed it on the fallen buildings. And they talked about the history of the font used in the postcards that said we're all in this together that were suddenly in all the postcard kiosks in the bathrooms of restaurants and bars. They talked about the friend who showed up at Halloween dressed as Mullah Omar and they wondered if this was in bad taste or if it could possibly have a certain ironic lightness. They talked about who else was with who else and for how long and whether it was a mating that made sense or one that made no sense at all. And they talked about the subway and how it still did not really work and they bragged about various subway rides they had to do in the last months and told mythic stories about times when the trains were so screwed up that they had to take four trains just to get from one island to the next island.

At the gatherings they drank too much as was usual to do with or without the falling buildings. And they laughed too loud as was usual to do when they drank too much. And they made passes at each other as was usual to do when drinking too much and laughing too loud. And they had affairs as a result of making passes as always happens but this time they blamed it on the buildings being gone and their resulting disorientation, their sudden difficulty in figuring out what was north and what was south. Sometimes they were forgiven by their partners and sometimes relationships shuffled and reconfigured in the way that they were shuffling and reconfiguring even in times of calmness and somewhat clean air.

While at both the readings and the gatherings they felt that what mattered were the certain specific conversations they were having with each other, conversations that would go on late into the night and would be defined by seriousness rather than lightness but would be unsummarizable and unmemorable the next day. While there was drunken laughing and drunken passes there was no drunken dancing. There was little screaming and if there was any screaming it was when they were angry about each other's politics and this screaming was yet another sign of how the readings and gatherings mattered to them in various ways or how the things they said at the readings and gatherings mattered or how the opinions that they held mattered to them. There was never any screaming in celebration at these gatherings or readings. Mainly there was just conversation. One-on-one conversation. While at the bar after the readings or at the gatherings, these conversations felt deeper than family. Felt resonant. As if they were shaping their lives. They felt that life was good as long as they could talk about the lyrics to Brandy with other people who also knew the lyrics to Brandy and had a relationship to them that was like theirs, that abandoned irony in the pursuit of all-out sentiment. The readings and the gatherings were a sort of ephemera that rose up when the buildings fell. They were a place to feel safe, to feel as if it were fine to be a pervert because they were with other perverts, those who identified as queer or not, the pagans and the abortionists and the feminists and the gays and the lesbians and the ACLU and the People for the American Way.

So there was a certain emotion in the air. This emotion was trivial. It was not an emotion that would last. It was a passing emotion. It was the emotion commonly experienced around brushes with disaster and the awareness of having been spared. The after a hurricane, after a black out, after a tornado, after an earthquake emotion. All of this gave the small parts of their lives the same intensity with which they listened to poetry. One night, standing in the cold out on the sidewalk looking at the towers-of-light while waiting for friends to come out of the bar, they realized that while the collapsing buildings did not cause them to fall in love, make babies, give rings to one another, settle down finally after years of having trouble with commitments, it did change the way they read poetry, the way they looked at art, the way they thought about ideas. Even before the buildings fell down, they had gone to many poetry readings. They went to poetry readings where poems that used fragmentation, quotation, disruption, disjunction, agrammatical syntax, and so on were read. On the odd occasion where the poets used complete sentences, they were usually used ironically. The fragmentation felt reassuring to them. Felt like a trance-inducing chant. Like a philosophy of connection. Like a model of intimacy that was full of acquaintances and publics that recognized not only points of contact and mixing, but also relational difficulties, cultural and linguistic difference. And so they often wondered in this time if perhaps all those who claimed that poetry was a comfort were right. Even if those who claimed this were usually talking about lyric poetry and not poetry that used fragmentation, quotation, disruption, disjunction, agrammatical syntax, and so on. They had noticed before that they felt writing in their body. That they felt those certain sensations, those sensations of interested calmness that happened when their mind and their breath were working together, that pleasant boredom. And they began at this time to think of the poetry that used fragmentation, quotation, disruption, disjunction, agrammatical syntax, and so on not as a radical avant-garde break but as the warm hand of someone they loved stroking their head, helping them to relax the muscles in their head and inviting them to just close their eyes and relax for a second with the words of someone else. This feeling somewhat answered that constant question of about the use of the avant-garde in a time like this.

9

During the time when the buildings fell and the time of the consequences of that, the time when words like asbestos, lead, mercury, dioxins, furans, hydrogen cyanide, benzene, xylene, chromium, polychlorinated biphenyls, aromatic hydrocarbons, and volatile organic compounds entered their daily conversations, the time of ghosts, the time when the fallen buildings caused people to fall in love, to make babies, to give rings to one another, to settle down finally after years of having trouble with commitments, the time in which they became even more embarrassed about being a pervert and hubristically afraid that it would be noticed and there would be consequences to this noticing, the time of various operations already happening and operations to come with names like Operation Lancer Lightning, Operation Vigilant Resolve, Operation Resolute Sword, Operation Danger Fortitude, Operation Ripper Sweep, Operation Yellow Stone, Operation Rapier Thrust, Operation Spring Clean-up, and Operation Striker Hurricane, they thought a lot about the ocean, the clear, warm part of the ocean that is near the island in the Pacific. They thought of salty water and the certain shades of blue that the ocean took on as it neared the equator. They thought over and over about immersing themselves in the water that surrounded the island in the Pacific. How they wanted to just sink down into the ocean. The ocean over their legs. The ocean over their stomach. The ocean over their chest. The ocean over their head. Then the feeling of not breathing and of hair floating out in the ocean. The feeling of not breathing in the awful smoke that was floating over the island in the Atlantic, that plume of smoke that looked beautiful in the satellite images on the internet but choked them with its fear and conservative values when they were in it.

They thought, in other words, that if people just went away it would no longer be the time when words like asbestos, lead, mercury, dioxins, furans, hydrogen cyanide, benzene, xylene, chromium, polychlorinated biphenyls, aromatic hydrocarbons, and volatile organic compounds entered their daily conversations, the time of ghosts, the time when the fallen buildings caused people to fall in love, to make babies, to give rings to one another, to settle down finally after years of having trouble with commitments, the time in which they became even more embarrassed about being a pervert and hubristically afraid that they would notice and there would be consequences to this noticing, the time of various operations already happening and operations to come with names like Operation Quarterhorse Rides, Operation Phantom Linebacker, Operation Cajun Mousetrap II, Operation Cajun Mousetrap III, Operation Iron Fury, Operation Iron Fury II, Operation Wolverine, Operation Clean Sweep, and Operation True Grit. This thought that things would be different if the humans just went away was probably true. But the disappearance of all humans was of course impossible for them to induce and they wouldn't even induce it if they could. They liked humans, liked their contradictions. Still when things got too intense, they spent a lot of time thinking absurdly about the island in the middle of the Pacific as an unpopulated island and they also spent a lot of time looking at the plume of smoke from the still-burning buildings on the internet because no people were evident in the satellite images. Basically, they wanted to be lost, away from the burning, away from the retribution and the killing that was already happening or was going to happen, organized by the government that currently occupied the continent, and that would have or already had names like Operation Outlaw Destroyer, Operation Haifa Street, Operation Mutual Security, Operation Tombstone Pile Driver, Operation Mayfield III, Operation Cobra Sweep, Operation Showdown, Operation Grizzly Forced Entry, and Operation Warrior Resolve. But they knew at the same time that the island in the middle of the Pacific was also occupied by the military that currently occupied the continent and that thoughts of the ocean that surrounded the island in the middle of the Pacific were in no way a rational escape and also all the technology that let them look at the island in the Atlantic as a beautiful plume of smoke existed because of the military.

The killing that was already happening or was going to happen hung over them heavily in this time. It moved into their apartment and lived with them. They were intimate and involved with it. It was an unwanted lover, one that was ruining the relationships they saw as real and yet they could not end this relationship they had with the killing that was already happening or was going to happen. One afternoon one of them said it didn't matter whether they lived apart or together because they had their whole lives to live together. When they said this, a small off-the-cuff comment that they might not even have meant, they felt at this moment the whole room darken and they felt their bodies grow smaller and smaller in this darkness that surrounded them. Hearing this hit them in the gut and made them overwhelmed with a huge sadness and they thought suddenly with longing of all the comfort they got from their nights moving between the softer bed with its room in another room that had no light from the outside that entered it and the harder bed with its room full of light and a tree outside the window that had various city birds who sang city birdsongs in the morning. And they replied, crying, there are soldiers moving to the borders and who knows what they might do and because of this they had to live their lives in the same place, sleep near each other. Something about this offhand comment took them over and reminded them of their vulnerability. And then once they thought of their vulnerability and how it was induced by the thought of the killing that was already happening or was going to happen by the government that currently occupied the continent and would have or already had names like Operation Wolfpack Crunch, Operation Disarm, Operation Giuliani, Operation Slim Shady, Operation Striker Tornado, Operation Rocketman III, Operation Dragon Victory, Operation Gimlet Crusader, and Operation Gimlet Silent Sniper, they thought also of how absurd their feeling was because they were so protected from this killing that the government that currently occupied the continent did in their name even though the buildings had fallen down less than a mile away while they stood on the street corner watching it happen. And at that moment a small sliver of an awareness of how vulnerable those who lived in other places, those places where the killing that was caused by the government that currently occupied the continent and would have or already had names like Operation New Market, Operation Lightning, Operation Moon River Dragon, Operation Spear (Rohme), Operation Sword (Saif), Operation Muthana Strike, Operation Bow Country, Operation Scimitar, and Operation Warrior's Rage must have felt entered into their bodies and paralyzed them with sadness and a strong sense of their ineffectiveness.

All around them they saw the signs of even more killing coming. They went one day to the store to buy boots because they had to go to a place where it often snowed and they found out that combat boots were hard to get because the military that currently occupied the continent on which they lived was buying them in such great numbers. This was just one sign among many signs that even more killing was coming. Among the most obvious was that it was not unusual to go into a bar and to hear they who were drinking beers in the afternoon calling for even more killing. And it was not just they in the bar and on the streets calling for even more killing, not just they who lived in the city where the buildings had fallen down, the city that was now full of awful smoke and anthrax and ghosts and soldiers from the military that currently occupied the continent, they who were likely and understandably to have intense and confused emotions during this time. But also calling for even more killing were some of their fellow poets. At this time the world felt divided between two types of humans: they who wanted an end to killing and they who wanted even more killing. And because some they had respected or at least had seen for years as having a certain political sensibility such as a poet who was a self-proclaimed lefty who had been involved in grassroots organizing for years, a critic who was devoted to work that used fragmentation, quotation, disruption, disjunction, agrammatical syntax, and so on, another poet who was prickly and intense in their hatred of hierarchical systems, were all calling for more killing very vocally in various e-mail messages to various discussion listserves or in letters to the editor of various prominent newspapers, they didn't know as as a result who they were, who they could trust.

They were caught in this disorientation and were spun around by it all day long. They were not necessarily pacificists. They valued resistance. And they valued armed resistance. They felt, for instance, that they on the planes as passengers should have killed they who were driving the planes into buildings. They thought that those who were on the continent and islands before the ships from afar arrived and claimed the lands and then set up their own form of government were right to take up arms and fight this takeover. And they thought this even though they avoided shooting guns and did not really like them all that much and were unlikely to join an armed resistance. But they could not extend this to the idea that the military that currently occupied the continent should bomb they in another place because some other they that lived in the same place might have had something to do with the they who drove the planes into the buildings. Nation was mainly repulsive to them. And in this instance it was worse than repulsive.

They continued during this time to feel the news heavily, feel it in their bodies as a virus that was irritating and infecting the wound torn open by the fallen buildings. They still didn't, couldn't, understand much. Or rather it was that they refused to understand much because the understanding was too horrible and so instead of being horrified with understanding they adopted a pose of false naïveté and would go around saying things in the simplest of terms, ignoring all the endless reasons that were obvious for everything that happened. So they would say that all they knew was that a number of buildings had collapsed recently; that all they knew was that the force of hundreds of floors falling one after another on top of one another had also fallen on a whole lot of ideas they valued and then smoke had risen up that was heavy and thick with fear and conservative values. If they did not say falsely naïve things like this then they would have to be listing all those facts that they had heard called out into the apartment after the buildings fell. They would have to be listing the number killed over the years by the military that currently occupied the continent as a result of bombings, the number killed by probable indirect causes, the number killed by coups supported by the military that currently occupied the continent, the number killed by arms sold by companies based on the continent, the number killed by technologies developed by companies based on the continent.

One afternoon while they on the island in the Atlantic lay on their bed thinking purposefully naïve thoughts, they realized that they were sweating and that it was ninety degrees in April. It would not have surprised them if it was ninety degrees in April if they were on the island in the middle of the Pacific, but the island in the Atlantic had four seasons and April was a cold, wet one. This ninety degrees in April was making it hard for them to maintain their purposive naïveté.

And because it was April the daffodils that the city of Stuttgart had sent after the buildings had fallen were blooming. But because it was ninety degrees in April, the daffodils suddenly died. The daffodils that were supposed to be a memorial to the fallen buildings, a mundane bright ray of hope, instead became a memorial to how the weather was changing because of the devotion the government that currently occupied the continent had to oil. In March the Larsen B ice shelf of the Antarctic Peninsula had collapsed. They did not know this happened until

April but once they read the news story on the internet they watched the glacier crack in a series of time-lapse photographs over and over. It was this cracking of the Larsen B ice shelf that turned them from making charts of killings as a result of bombings, charts of probable indirect killings, charts of killings done by coups supported by the government that currently occupied the continent, charts of killings done by arms sold by companies based on the continent, charts of killings done by technologies developed by companies based in the continent, to listing the changes in the environment. To do this, they set up a special e-mail account and they got up each morning and read the news, the same news that the program that one of them made would be scrambling, and they e-mailed themselves articles about the environment. Their e-mail account collected articles about the one thousand eight hundred and fifty-six threatened species of the world's amphibians, about the one hundred and sixty-eight probably extinct amphibian species, and about the ninety percent plunge in the population of large ocean fish. They added detail after detail to the e-mail account. The massive die-off of an estimated thirty-four thousand chinook, coho, and steelhead salmon on the Klamath River near the California-Oregon border. The 10 percent drop in sunshine reaching the surface of the Earth over the last forty years and even how in some major industrialized cities the sunlight had decreased as much as 37 percent. The disappearing belt of Irish moss. The list went on and on. The weakening Atlantic currents. The unprecedented rise in carbon dioxide, methane, and nitrous oxide. The outbreaks of algae that destroyed coral reefs and were caused by overfishing. The Pacific Gray whale's inability to find enough fatty amphipods. The dust that was blowing across the expanding Sahara to Trinidad. The parts of the San Francisco bay where 99 percent of the species are invasive. The miconia covering the Big Island. The 70 percent reduction of the zooplankton biomass. The salmon streams at temperatures unsafe for spawning. The lengthening mosquito season. The nitrogen-based fertilizers destroying the Great Barrier reef. The 97 percent of southern bluefin tuna gone and high mercury concentrations in those that remain.

But despite the e-mail account and its subject headings that indicated environmental collapse in all sorts of different areas, it was glaciers that caught their imagination and obsessed them. They were so big, so sparkly, such a huge and easy metaphor. And when climate change was modeled it always seemed as if the disaster started with the ice caps melting. And then what happened after that—whether the Gulf Stream would fail or not, whether the earth would return to the temperatures of the Altithermal or the Eemian or the much scarier Paleocene-Eocene thermal maximum, whether things would get dramatically hotter or dramatically colder once the ice caps melted and a series of unknown systemic changes began, whether they would be under water or if there would be no water—was open to debate. So they set up another e-mail account for glaciers and they began e-mailing themselves article after article about disappearing glaciers. Articles about how Iceland's Vatnajokull glacier is melting by about three feet a year. About the Bering Glacier in Alaska, which had recently lost as much as twelve kilometers in a sixty-day period. About the European Alps, which had lost half their ice over the last century, and the fact that many of the rivers of Europe were likely to be gone in twenty to thirty years. About the Columbia Glacier in Alaska which is likely to continue to recede, possibly at a rate of as much as ten miles in ten years. About the thirty-six cubic miles of ice that had melted from glaciers in West Antarctica in the past decade and that alone had raised sea levels worldwide by about one-sixtieth of an inch. About Mt. Rainier, which was having something called glacial outbursts that happen only when warm temperatures melt ice under the glacier, forcing water to suddenly burst out of the ground and race down the mountain. About the tropical ice caps that were disappearing even faster. About the glacier on the Quelccaya ice cap, which was retreating by one hundred and fifty-five meters per year. About the Kilimanjaro in East Africa, which had lost 82 percent of its area in eighty-eight years. About the predications that the Artic system is heading to an ice-free state in summer. About the possible collapse of the Greenland ice sheet. About the Artic average temperature rising at almost twice the rate of the rest of the world. About the Portage Glacier losing twenty feet a year.

They learned that all this melting began to accelerate in 1988. That the rate of ice lost had doubled since 1988. They thought then about how they had been alive in 1988, which was for a few years the warmest year on record. They knew that that year they had thought little about the weather. They had spent the summer living in various parts of the continent. None of them knew each other at that moment. And they thought of them each in different places on the continent going about doing the things they did without an awareness that a hot period was beginning to accelerate. That year, they worried about different things. About starting college. About finishing college. About getting a job. Or they thought about hitting baseballs. Or they were trying to rid themselves of drunk partners by not returning any of their phone calls and eventually not listening to any of the messages they left on their machine late at night in a voice full of drunkenness and deep sadness. Or they were not mowing their lawn and letting it grow long and have dandelions that made the neighbors complain but they saw as a sign of their antiauthoritarian, laid-back style. Perhaps they had sushi for the first time that year. And they probably all left their windows open at night in various different parts of the continent that summer, some of them pressing their sweaty bodies against others of them and others of them sleeping alone. They were undoubtedly full of emotion and contentment and discontentment in that year and assuredly thinking only about themselves. They were full of living and their hearts beat singularly and were strong in their bodies. And they did all of this or variations of all of this without any thoughts of the melting arctic ice, without any thoughts of what that heat that summer meant. It had appeared at the time without the anxiety of climate change. That summer they had only noticed that it was hot. Not that a series of climatic events that were complicated and cascading was beginning.

But now as they read on the internet late at night, their eyes blurring, their shoulders tired, they realized that they could see so many hottest years on record after 1988. And they then started collecting articles about the hottest year on record. After 1988, there was 1995. Then there was 1997. And then 1998. And it went on and on. The articles were all the same. They began with at one time some recent other year had been the hottest year. But now it had been determined that this year was the hottest year. Year after year they could read the same article with more or less the same language but with different years.

Sometimes as they read on the internet late at night they found arguments from the side that the oil drillers and oil sellers upheld. The side that said the melting did not matter. Sometimes, if it was really late at night and they had written on a small notepad beside their computer an especially long list of things that were melting, they would read this argument by oil drillers and oil sellers and try to be reassured by the information that if the Antarctic Pine Island glacier melted away it didn't matter much because it would raise sea levels only by a quarter of an inch. A quarter of an inch they would think. A quarter of an inch does not matter. Then the obvious questions would surface through this blurry comfort of small amounts. Would the Pine Island glacier melt just on its own, they would wonder? Or would the Vatnajokull join it? And then the alps and then the tropical ice caps and then the poles? And then they read that while a quarter of an inch does not seem like much, a rise of one foot of ocean level typically means that shorelines end up one hundred feet or more inland. A sea rise of just three feet in Bangladesh would put half of that nation underwater, displacing more than one hundred million people. Already on many of the islands and atolls of the southern Pacific they must grow their plants in containers because the rising sea level has seeped into the ground water.

Basically they gave in to every tidbit of environmental information they could find so they could stop thinking so hard about the asbestos, lead, mercury, dioxins, furans, hydrogen cyanide, benzene, xylene, chromium, polychlorinated biphenyls, aromatic hydrocarbons, and volatile organic compounds in the air, about the operations that had already happened or were going to happen that had names like Operation Black Typhoon, Operation Hurricane, Operation Hurricane II, Operation Iron Fist 2, Operation Longhorn, Operation Blue Tiger, Operation Baton Rouge, Operation Phantom Fury, and Operation Bulldog. And they combined this with an absurd aesthetic devotion to the flora and fauna and something about the fact that it was all disappearing made them treasure it all the more. Often they lay around the house in the afternoon pursuing their false naïveté by watching nature shows on the television. Or they would imagine themselves hovering over the land and noticing the dendritic, trellis, pinnate, parallel, radial, and rectangular patterns that rivers and their networks of tributaries make and then they in their minds zoomed in and noticed the wind and current patterns in the sand on various beaches and deserts, patterns with clear repetitive features that at the same time lacked a strict periodicity, and then they zoomed out again and hovered over the physiographical uneven and meandering configurations of the shoreline, and then they swooped back down and noticed the play between inwardly and outwardly branching patterns in various seaweeds, and then they flipped over and noticed the amorphous boundaries and turbulent structures of the clouds.

As they collected this information, as they hovered and zoomed and flipped, they lived their lives as a series of contradictions. In their house they had hour-long discussions about how best to compost and then they would go out and buy a hamburger packaged in a thick plastic disposable container from the take-out restaurant on the corner. They would buy dish soap that was marketed as ecologically friendly in a plastic bottle and then they would run the water constantly as they did the dishes. They wrote poems in which they remembered the ocean and then they would fly on planes that spewed out the contrails that were increasing the cirrus coverage and thus contributing significantly to warming to read these poems to small audiences who already were concerned with the ocean and did not need the reminder. They ran their computer for hours while they searched the internet for evidence of environmental destruction. They stopped eating most seafood because the ocean was overfished but allowed themselves to eat squid because they read that as the ocean warmed their territory and numbers were increasing. In other words, they did not even try to be innocent. They did not even do the obvious things they could do. It was as if when they had moved to an island in the middle of the Pacific and had become infected with the prickly new cells, they could now see the huge amount of historical data and position that they carried with them and they could not stop seeing it. They could not stop thinking about where they should put their bodies on the planet and because there was no right answer they were caught in a feedback loop and so they remembered the ocean so they could give the gray matter at the back of their brain a rest. They remembered the ocean and with the ocean they remembered the land and the air, as a respite from politics, a respite from cultural politics, from sexual politics, from identity politics, from national politics. They had to admit it. They turned to the pastoral so they could escape the endless back and forth of all these politics, a back and forth that kept them at the computer late at night looking for some truth, some pattern, amongst all the information. For years they had worried various politics. They had worried cultural politics, sexual politics, identity politics, and national politics as if they were a loose tooth that had yet to come out. As if they liked the pain, liked the way the tooth felt loose in their mouth, liked the blood that came as they moved it back and forth. So they hovered and zoomed and flipped in pursuit of aesthetic pleasures, in pursuit of uneven patterns and variable repetitions. But the more they hovered and zoomed and flipped the more the prickly new cells took over and they could no longer enjoy the wind and current patterns in the sand without also thinking of how human-induced desertification threatens nearly a quarter of land surface of the planet. Still there were so many moments where they looked around and recognized that the world was a place of stunning beauty even now amidst the melting and desertifying. Stunning, stunning beauty.

When it came down to it, it was an awkward time and it was the awkwardness that obsessed them. It was an awkward time for them and for the word them. It was a time of overt and dramatically unsustainable resource use. It was a time of oil. And because it was a time of oil, it was a time of risk. It was a time of an altered environment, an environment altered by the oil economy. It was a time of invasive species. A time of climate change. A time of an overly fished and empty ocean. A time of the elimination of predators from ecosystems. A time of toxins in the water. A time of not enough fresh water. A time when it seemed all the parts of the world were being turned into an oil-based indestructible plastic. And because of this it was a time of bombing in different parts of the world. A great deal of this bombing was done by the military that currently occupied the continent. And in order for there to be bombing there had to be a we and a they, an us and a them. So it was a time of troubled and pressured pronouns.

And because it was an awkward time, they had to agree to be awkward. When they had met in a bar and agreed to move to an island in the middle of the Pacific together, they had agreed to attempt a small transformation of some sort. They did not know the result of the transformation or what to call the transformation but they had agreed to it nonetheless. They agreed then to be enthralled with each other. They agreed to let the story they told about themselves as individuals be interrupted by others. They agreed to let their speech be filled with signs of each other and their enthrallment and their undoing. They agreed to falter over pronouns. They agreed to let them undo their speech and language. They pressed themselves upon them and impinged upon them and were impinged upon in ways that were not in their control.

At that moment, they had agreed to a third point, a Sapphic point. And because of this third Sapphic point, they did not look into each others eyes with the assumption of a direct return that would then let them forget the world around them. They agreed to no longer see relationship as a feedback loop of face-to-face desire. Instead they had to deal with a sort of shimmering, a fracturing of all their looks and glances. And it was because of this third Sapphic point that they implicated themselves in they. They could have, should have, come to this third Sapphic point on their own even if they had not one afternoon met in a bar and decided to fix their relationship into a triangle. They could have, should have, come to this on their own because it was an awkward time. Many others around them realized this on their own. But they were slow to see how awkward the time was because they lived in such privilege and it took an adjustment to their intimacies to get them to realize how much they were a they.

At times when they spoke of them and also to them they were not clear about when they were doing which or what they was what, but still they gave themselves over to they. And they talked to each other as if they were they. As if they each had brain stems of their own but the brain stems were connected to each other and if they all took the same drug they would all arrive together on the other side of the blood brain barrier and be there in some other space, just there, talking about nothing or about something. They just wanted to talk to each other the way that humans talk to each other when they go on long car trips in the country and they have nothing really to say after the first hour in the car but sometimes in the hours that follow they might point something out or talk some about what thoughts came to them as they drove along, mesmerized by the blur of space passing by them. They wanted to be they the way that humans might be they with a dog and a dog they with humans, intimately together yet with a limited vocabulary. They wanted to be they like blood cells are compelled to be a they. What they meant was that they were other than completely autonomous but they were not one thing with no edges, with no boundary lines.

They felt they could not allow themselves to be an us. That they had to be a they. And when they thought rationally they felt that being they in this awkward time should have made them feel more safe. There was after all more of them. They should have felt more protected. They had not only another but also anothers in the third Sapphic point, in the domestic space. And they knew also that they were fine, that life was fine, with the one-on-one or the face-to-face of the beloved and the lover. That other formation. It was fine, even if the world around them was awkward, both ways. So they had more than enough. They had excess.

But the opposite happened. Once they became attached to each other, their lives intertwined and the more they grew into each other they felt their attachment to each other in their twining limbs and in their fluttering seed parts as a risk. Because there were more of them than they were used to, there was more to lose. It was as if once they felt attachment, that same feeling of attachment opened them up to a whole new series of worries and they had to worry not only about themselves but also about those attachments and then about those to whom they were attached. Or it was that they were at risk of losing their attachments the moment they admitted they had attachments and this changed how they thought of things. The more attachments they had, the more that could possibly be lost in this unstable time, the more parts of them that might be in some falling building, the more parts of them that might be called upon to bomb other parts of them, the more risk that their third Sapphic point might be recognized as being against those values of oil, the values of singular attachments that so defined the government that currently occupied the continent at this time and even though this thought was clearly irrational and risked foolishness with its hubris in the way of all paranoia, they still thought it.

They were in this time defined by heart-thumping anxiety. It was as if they needed at least two hearts in their body, maybe more. They had parts of themselves that contradicted and they needed the bones of their ribs broken and then their chest cracked open and then for someone to go in and add at least one more heart and then sew them together with a needle and thread. What would be left would be a thick scar and an uneven beat. They needed to become monstrous in their heart. This becoming monstrous they knew was only a beginning but it felt necessary. That singular organ needed to be made bigger. They need to bring things inside of them that shouldn't be inside of them.

It was not the third Sapphic point but the endless worrying and e-mail accounts that made them need this monstrous heart. How they looked one way and saw the one or the other. Then how they looked another way and saw the one and the other. How they were torn between philosophies of coming together and staying apart. They could see that both philosophies of coming together and staying apart had their uses and their limits. And often parts of them combined in the same system in a sort of push-me-pull-me dynamic. And they felt they could get nowhere until they let both of them into their bodies by which they meant into the palm of their writing hand, in that space that their little and ring fingers made when they held a pen, the space that when they were learning to write in first grade they had been forced to fill with a small cool marble so as to learn the proper way to hold a pencil. And to make sense of this push-me-pull-me game of coming together and staying apart with the palm of their writing hand, they had to let both coming together and staying apart into their hearts as a dynamic. They could not write about the 70 percent reduction of the ocean's zooplankton biomass without having one-way tickets for haoles off the island in their heart and they could not write about one-way tickets for haoles off the island without having the impositions of imperialisms and an understanding of how their legacies continued to shape them in their heart and they could not write the impositions of imperialisms and their legacies without having the third Sapphic point in their heart and they could not write about the third Sapphic point without having the expansionist language in their heart and they could not write about the expansionist language without having the arrival of the huehue haole in their heart and they could not write about the arrival of the huehue haole without the air from the fallen buildings that made them retch in their heart and they could not write about the air from the fallen buildings that made them retch without having the ghosts and the DNA in the dust in their heart and they could not write about the ghosts and the DNA in the dust without having the operations that were already happening and operations to come with names like Operation Devil Thrust, Operation Aloha, Operation Centaur Rodeo, Operation Warrior, Operation Suicide Kings, Operation Tiger Fury, Operation Iron Saber, Operation Duke Fortitude, Operation Lancer Fury, and Operation Lancer Lighting in their heart and they could not write about the operations that were already happening and operations to come with names like Operation Rock Bottom, Operation Falcon Freedom, Operation Soprano Sunset, Operation Wonderland, Operation Powder River, Operation Triple Play, Operation Therapist, Operation Lanthonid, and Operation Copperas Cove without having the 70 percent reduction in the ocean's zooplankton biomass in their heart. They realized at this moment that they had to stop making maps that were limited by their horizontal or vertical axes. Or charts that started with two options and then spread from there. They need a new sort of conceptualization that allowed for more going astray than any map they had ever seen.

So they began to pump through these new hearts without thought or discrimination or rationality about their limits all they could with the hope that it would eventually reach the palm of their writing hand. They pumped milkweed and butterfly through their superior vena cavas. Then they pumped through their right atriums the uncountable number of species. Through their tricuspid valves they pumped a connective hope and a connective paranoia and an acknowledgement that most days they chose connective paranoia, by which they meant that they chose to hear the names of the operations that were already happening and operations to come with names like Operation Checkmate, Operation River Blitz, Operation Fontana, Operation Badlands, Operation Forsyth Park, Operation Cobweb, Operation Matador, Operation Peninsula, and Operation Squeeze Play because to know these names felt like a sort of hope finally, a hope that they could not explain. They let the names of the passiflora pass through their right ventricles. And then they let into their pulmonic valves the species lost each day, the named and noticed species and the species not yet named or not yet noticed. Let in health and in sickness into their pulmonary arteries. And then let their heart pump to their lungs the awkward bodies of a five-hour time difference after a ten-hour flight. And then around again, they moved from their lungs to their pulmonary veins elaborate charts of things that confused them. And let the issue of belonging hit them in the palm of their writing hand and through their left atriums. And let into their mitral valves a love of the land and a love of the things on the land, a love of how the kukui clustered in veinlike streams down the crevice of a ravine, a love of heart-shaped velvety leaves that undulated from graceful stalks in a soft breeze, a love of the varieties of squeaks, whistles, rasping notes, and clicking sounds of the 'i'iwi. And they passed through their left ventricles the winds and their many names in the langage that was on the island before the whaling ships arrived. Pumped through their aortic valves and into the palm of their writing hand the reminder that they wrote as war machine because there was no other way to write. And then vowed with their aortas to remember they also wrote as ideological state apparatus, as military-industrial complex, as colonial educational system, as the bulldozing of the land and the building of unnecessary roads, as the filling in of wetlands with imported sand to build beaches, and also as the ever-expanding tourist industry. They pumped through their bodies stumbling forward. And they then switched to another of their hearts and they let a tad too dark lipstick, a tad too short skirt, a tad too thick soles of shoes, and a tad too obvious writing pump through their aortas. Then they pumped through their aortic valves land snails that might have arrived on the island by a prehistoric chain of stepping-stone islands. And through their left ventricles honeycreepers—the 'i'iwi and the 'apapane and the 'ākohekohe. Pumped through their mitral valves hurricane winds that carried spores, seeds, and insects. And through their left atriums the migratory paths of the ruddy turnstone, the wandering tattlers, the sanderling, the pintail duck, and the shoveler duck. Through their pulmonary veins the spinelike pattern of reds and greens and yellows in the croton's leaf. Pumped through their lungs the back of the bus. And let in their pulmonary arteries the realization that they could only be colonizers who perpetuated even if they wanted to be colonizers who refused. They let their pulmonary arteries be under the sign of contradiction. They pumped the cracking Larsen B ice shelf through their right ventricles. Pumped through their tricuspid valves avenues and streets, the lines of bridges and the dialogue that the uneven heights of buildings in a row had with the air above them. And then in their right atriums, filled space and empty space. Pumped with the inferior vena cava endless nameless and faceless deaths. Pumped through the superior vena cava the losses in the world caused by the military that currently occupied the continent. Pumped back around with the inferior vena cavas all that they ate. And then pumped through their right atriums the expansionist language. Pumped with their tricuspid valves a vow to not think of themselves as separate from those killed by the military that currently occupied the continent or the grieving families of those killed by the military that currently occupied the continent. Pumped with the right ventricles the 70 percent reduction of the zooplankton biomass. Pumped through their pulmonic valves a theory of collective responsibility. Pumped with the pulmonary arteries a vow to let the nameless and faceless deaths caused by the military that currently occupied the continent break up their language. Pumped through their lungs grief for all of them killed by the military that currently occupied the continent, the thems they knew to be near them and the thems they knew not to be near them, because to not grieve meant that their humanity was at risk. Then back around to another heart, through the pulmonary veins they pumped long sentences and lists of connections, both paranoid and optimistic. Pumped with the left atriums attempts to map things out through writing so as to understand them. Pumped through the mitral valves the words of others. Pumped with the left ventricles the admission that they didn't have any real answers, only the hope that if they kept writing others might point them to answers. Pumped through the aortic valves changes. With grief, with worry, with desire, with attachment, with anything and everything, they began listing, inventorying, recognizing in the hope that a catalogue of vulnerability could begin the process of claiming their being human, claiming the being human of their perverse third Sapphic point, claiming the being human of the space in the palm of their writing hand, in that space that their little and ring fingers made when they held a pen, the space that when they were learning to write in first grade they had been forced to fill with a small cool marble so as to learn the proper way to hold a pencil.

afterword

I have written this book over the last seven years now. I started it when I lived in Hawai'i. I'm not sure of the exact date. Maybe sometime in 1999 or 2000. Maybe earlier. An early version of this book is published in the online journal *How2* in 2001 in a section of new writing edited by Renee Gladman. I remember starting this book under the spell of both Gladman's and Pamela Lu's work. Both came to read in Hawai'i in 1999 or 2000 and so their sentences were on my mind.

This book tells a barely truthful story of the years 1997–2001. The most obvious way that it is barely truthful is that I have altered personal timelines. I lived in Hawai'i from August 1997 to August 2001. During this time I worked at the University of Hawai'i at Mānoa. I took a leave without pay in 2001 and moved to New York in August of that year not really planning to return. My plan was to become marginally employed. 9/11 made even marginal employment difficult in New York so I then moved back to Hawai'i in July 2002. This book does not follow me back to Hawai'i but it does tell stories from that 2002–2003 year as if they happened prior to August 2001, and as I worked on this book from 1999 to 2006, events from those years also worked their way into the narrative.

I have also altered other people's stories. I have split people in half and I have joined them together. Sometimes deliberately. Sometimes by accident. I have at moments changed people. At other moments I have let them be obvious.

Bill Luoma and Charles Weigl very patiently read this book, tolerated their misrepresentation and assimilation into it, and still helped me with sentence structure. David Buuck and Stephanie Young did detailed and attentive close readings of the manuscript and suggested tremendously helpful changes. My debt to both of them is huge. Kevin Davies did an instense proofreading. Jenny Lion rearranged paragraphs and made other suggestions. Susan Schultz usefully and generously argued with me about a number of issues. I also owe conversational debts on the Hawai'i material to Candace Ah Nee, Cindy Franklin, Emelihter Kihleng, Kyle Koza, Laura Lyons, Caroline Sinavaiana, Ida Yoshinaga, and John Zuern. I thank all of them, but, again, do not assume that they would tell the stories I tell here in the same way.

I have also stolen a lot. Sometimes whole sentences and descriptions of things got absorbed and sometimes rewritten and sometimes not. I did not keep good track of whom I stole from over the years that I wrote this book. But because this is an attempt at a barely truthful story, I will confess some of them, the ones I remember.

In the first section . . . Chris Daniels helped me with the word maracujá. The language about the passiflora's solar panels unfolding to the sun is stolen from Passiflora Online, www.passionflow.co.uk. The public television documentary is *The Life of Birds*, by David Attenborough. The music channel's soap opera is *Undressed*. The documentary is *The Marrying Tribe of the Amazon* and it is about the Zoé tribe. The phrase "cruel inquisitive they" comes from W. H. Auden via the *OED* and the sentences around this phrase in the book incorporate parts of the *OED* definitions for the words "complicity" and "they." The milkweed description comes from *The Jepson Desert Manual: Vascular Plants of Southeastern California*, edited by Bruce G. Baldwin, Steve Boyd, Barbara J. Ertter, Robert W. Patterson, Thomas J. Rosatti, and Dieter H. Wilken. The film about the decades-long love triangle is *Jules et Jim* (directed by François Truffaut, 1962).

Throughout this book, but especially in the first half of the book, the information on Hawai'i's plants and animals draws extensively from E. S. Craighill Handy and Elizabeth Green Handy with the collaboration of Mary Kawena Pukui's *Native Planters in Old Hawaii: Their Life, Lore, and Environment* (Honolulu: Bishop Museum Press, 1972). This book includes the sentence about the land snails, the honeycreepers, the koa, and the migratory animals. Some of the language about the mullet is also from this book. I'm also indebted to Isabella Aiona Abbott's *La'au Hawaii: Traditional Hawaiian Uses of Plants* (Honolulu: Bishop Museum Press, 1992). And also from a course in ethnobotany that I took at the University of Hawai'i at Mānoa that was taught by Alvin Chock. In addition, I spent a lot of time with Gerald Carr's various botany websites, especially his one on Hawaiian Native Plant Genera, http://www.botany.hawaii.edu/faculty/carr/natives.htm.

In the second section . . . The novelist who talks about the sea of islands is Epeli Hau'ofa in his essay "Our Sea of Islands," *The*

Contemporary Pacific 6 (1994): 148–161. The documentary on the atoll is *Rising Waters Global Warming and the Fate of the Pacific Islands*, produced, directed, and written by Andrea Torrice in 2000. William Blake's "The Tyger" begins with a line about fearful symmetry. This phrase though is really thanks to a conversation with Sianne Ngai about difficult feelings.

In the fourth section . . . The theorized writing about how the colonized live under the sign of a contradiction is Albert Memmi's *The Colonizer and the Colonized* (Boston: Beacon Press, 1991). I have used several other phrases from his work in this book. Among the many places where the haole schoolteacher shows up are Lois Ann Yamanaka's and Sia Figail's novels. Césaire writes about the mediocre colonizer in *Discourse on Colonialism* (tr. Joan Pinkham, New York University Press, 2000). I have an intense memory of reading this shortly after arriving in Hawai'i and gulping with self-recognition when I came to it. I wrote the parts of this chapter that are about creative writing in universities for a conference that Walter Lew did for Contemporary and Interdisciplinary Research in Asia called "Poetry, Pedagogy, and Alternative Internationalisms: From the Early 20th Century to the Present." Mark Nowak also presented a paper about creative writing and universities and reading his paper while writing my own was helpful (his paper was eventually published as ¡*Workers of the Word, Unite and Fight!* [Long Beach: Palm Press, 2006]). Huanani-KayTrask writes that her writing is a "furious, but nurturing *aloha*" in "Writing in Captivity: Poetry in a Time of Decolonization," in *Navigating Islands and Continents: Conversations and Contestations in and around the Pacific*, ed. Cynthia Franklin, Ruth Hsu, and Suzanne Kosanke (Honolulu: University of Hawai'i Press, 2000).

In the fifth section . . . The passages on the expansionist language draws from many sources, such as Daniel Nettle and Suzanne Romaine's *Vanishing Voices: The Extinction of the World's Languages* (New York: Oxford University Press, 2000) and Gilles Deleuze and Félix Guattari's reading of Kafka in *Kafka: Towards a Minor Literature* (tr. Dana Polan. Minneapolis: University of Minnesota Press, 1986). The language of English as a cultural bomb draws from Ngũgĩ wa Thiong'o in *Decolonising the Mind: The Politics of Language in African Literature* (Portsmouth: Heinemann, 1986). Trask's "Racist White Woman" is in *Light in the Crevice Never Seen* (Corvallis: Calyx Books, 1994, 67–68). I stole the term 747 poems from Rob Wilson's essay "From the Sublime to the Devious, Writing the Experimental/Local Pacific in Hawai'i," *boundary 2* 28, no. 1 (2001) 121–151. The koa'e bird poem is "Electric Lava" by Ku'ualoha Meyer Ho'omanawanui in *'Ōiwi* 1 (1998) 124–135. The song about the land in great danger is "Hawai'i 78" by Bruddah Iz. A version of this song is on the album *Iz: The Man and His Music* (1998, Mtn. Apple Co.). The creation chant is the *Kumulipo*. I used the Martha E. Beckwith translation (Honolulu: University of Hawai'i Press, 1981). Mai'a, 'ulu, kukui, and kī are often called canoe plants, basically plants that Polynesians brought with them as they traveled and then cultivated when they settled on an island. There is a decent introduction to these plants at www.canoeplants.com.

The list of operations that begin in the seventh section and continue to the end are from the website globalsecurity.org. Some of the information and language about the air in these same sections came from Juan González's *Fallout: The Environmental Consequences of the World Trade Center Collapse* (New York: Verso, 2003). Some of the information about bombing comes from Sven Lindqvist's *A History of Bombing* (tr. Linda Rugg; New York: Norton, 2003). The discussion on memorials in the seventh section owes debts to Judith Butler's *Antigone's Claim* (New York: Columbia University Press, 2002) and also to her *Precarious Life: The Power of Mourning and Violence* (New York: Verso, 2004).

In the seventh section . . . The language about the baboons comes from Natalie Angier's article "No Time for Bullies: Baboons Retool Their Culture" (*New York Times*, April 13, 2004).

In the eighth section . . . The poet who compared imperialism with perversion is Jack Hirschman in a reading at Naropa in 2005. The interview with the literary theorist known for her explorations of jouissance is an interview with Julia Kristeva that is collected in *Revolt, She Said* (New York: Semiotext(e), 2002). The poem that compares colonialism to getting fucked in the ass is "Host Culture (Guava Juice on a Tray)" by Māhealani Kamau'u in *'Ōiwi* 1 (1998), 135–136. It was on The 700 Club, on September 14, 2001 that Jerry Falwell said, "The abortionists have got to bear some burden for this because God will not be mocked. And when we destroy 40 million little innocent babies, we make God mad. I really believe that the pagans, and the abortionists, and the feminists, and the gays and the lesbians who are actively trying to make that an alternative lifestyle, the ACLU, People for the

American Way, all of them who have tried to secularize America, I point the finger in their face and say: you helped this happen." The poem with the office equipment is "The Dust" by Michael Gottlieb (eventually published in *Lost and Found* [New York: Roof Books, 2003]). The poem of one hundred and twenty-two stanzas is *Pain* by Alan Davies (New York: Other Publications, 2001). The poem written in five parts where each part uses only one vowel sound is Christian Bök's *Eunoia* (Toronto: Coach House Books, 2001). Kenneth Goldsmith's *Soliloquy* (New York: Granary, 2001) collects every word he spoke during the week of April 15–21, 1996.

In the ninth section . . . The third Sapphic point refers to the Mary Barnard version/translation of a Sappho fragment that she translates as "He is more than a hero" (*Sappho: A New Translation*, Berkeley: University of California Press, 1999) and also to Anne Carson's reading of this poem in *Eros: The Bittersweet* (Normal: Dalkey Archive, 1998).

Sections of this book have been published before. Thanks to the editors of *How2*, *Jubilat*, *Trout/Tinfish*, *Bay Poetics*, *Zyzzyva*, *No: A Journal of the Arts*, *Columbia Poetry*, and *Not Enough Night*. And as a chapbook under the title *Uneveness* [sic] (Philadelphia: Man Press, 2002). A great deal of work on this book got done during a year's leave I was able to take thanks to an American Council of Learned Societies fellowship. A Mills College Faculty Research grant and a Quigley Summer Research Grant from the Women's Studies Department also provided support.

Atelos was founded in 1995 as a project of Hip's Road and is devoted to publishing, under the sign of poetry, writing that challenges conventional, limiting definitions of poetry.

All the works published as part of the Atelos project are commissioned specifically for it, and each is involved in some way with crossing traditional genre boundaries, including, for example, those that would separate theory from practice, poetry from prose, essay from drama, the visual image from the verbal, the literary from the nonliterary, and so forth.

The Atelos project when complete will consist of 50 volumes.

The project directors and editors are Lyn Hejinian and Travis Ortiz. The director for text production and design is Travis Ortiz; the director for cover production and design is Ree Katrak.

Atelos (current volumes):

1. *The Literal World*, by Jean Day
2. *Bad History*, by Barrett Watten
3. *True*, by Rae Armantrout
4. *Pamela: A Novel*, by Pamela Lu
5. *Cable Factory 20*, by Lytle Shaw
6. *R-hu*, by Leslie Scalapino
7. *Verisimilitude*, by Hung Q. Tu
8. *Alien Tatters*, by Clark Coolidge
9. *Forthcoming*, by Jalal Toufic
10. *Gardener of Stars*, by Carla Harryman
11. *lighthouse*, by M. Mara-Ann
12. *Some Vague Wife*, by Kathy Lou Schultz
13. *The Crave*, by Kit Robinson

14. *Fashionable Noise*, by Brian Kim Stefans
15. *Platform*, by Rodrigo Toscano
16. *Tis of Thee*, by Fanny Howe
17. *Poetical Dictionary*, by Lohren Green
18. *Blipsoak01*, by Tan Lin
19. *The Up and Up*, by Ted Greenwald
20. *Noh Business*, by Murray Edmond
21. *Open Clothes*, by Steve Benson
22. *Occupational Treatment*, by Taylor Brady
23. *City Eclogue*, by Ed Roberson
24. *Ultravioleta*, by Laura Moriarty
25. *Negativity*, by Jocelyn Saidenberg
26. *The Transformation*, by Juliana Spahr

Distributed by:

Small Press Distribution
1341 Seventh Street
Berkeley, California
94710-1403

Atelos
P O Box 5814
Berkeley, California
94705-0814

to order from SPD call 510-524-1668 or toll-free 800-869-7553
fax orders to: 510-524-0852
order via e-mail at: orders@spdbooks.org
order online from: www.spdbooks.org

The Transformation
was first printed in an edition of 1200 copies
at Thomson-Shore, Inc.
A second printing of 750 copies,
and a third of 500 copies, followed.
This is the fourth printing, of 750 copies.
Text design and typesetting by Lyn Hejinian
using Goudy Oldstyle Hawaian for the text
and Caslon 224 Book for titles and subtitles.
Cover design by Ree Katrak / Great Bay Graphics.